United States
Department of
Agriculture

Forest Service

Pacific Northwest
Research Station

Resource Bulletin
PNW-RB-257

November 2008

Incidence of Insects, Diseases, and Other Damaging Agents in Oregon Forests

Paul Dunham

Author

Paul Dunham (retired) was a forest health analyst, U.S.Department of Agriculture. Forest Service, Forest Health Protection, Pacific Northwest Region, 333 SW First Avenue, Portland, OR 97204.

Abstract

Dunham, Paul A. 2008. Incidence of insects, diseases, and other damaging agents in Oregon forests. Resour. Bull. PNW-RB-257. Portland, OR: U.S. Department of Agriculture, Forest Service, Pacific Northwest Research Station. 89 p.

This report uses data from a network of forest inventory plots sampled at two points in time, annual aerial insect and disease surveys, and specialized pest damage surveys to quantify the incidence and impact of insects, diseases, and other damaging agents on Oregon's forests. The number and volume of trees damaged or killed by various agents is summarized. Differences in the frequency and severity of damaging agents between various ownership categories and geographic regions of the state are investigated.

Keywords: Forest surveys, forest inventory, forest insects, forest diseases, Oregon.

Summary

This report is a summary of the insects, diseases, and other tree-damaging agents that occur in Oregon forests and how they influence forest health. The data used to produce this report were compiled from Pacific Northwest Forest Inventory and Analysis (PNW-FIA) plots, the Pacific Northwest Region (Oregon and Washington national forests) inventory plots, the Bureau of Land Management (BLM) inventory plots, the U.S. Forest Service-Oregon Department of Forestry Aerial Survey Program aerial survey maps, and the USDA Forest Service Forest Health Monitoring Program-Oregon Department of Forestry balsam woolly adelgid survey. With the exception of park lands and private reserves, the plots used in this report are a systematic sample of all Oregon forests sampled at two points in time. Key findings are:

- Slightly over one-third of live trees sampled have some sort of damage from insects, diseases, or other causes. The most common damages recorded were physical injuries such as dead tops, basal scars, and forks.

- Trees east of the crest of the Cascade range were about twice as likely to have some sort of damage as trees in the west.

- Aside from unknown causes and physical injuries, the most commonly recorded causes of mortality were bark beetles and root diseases with 19 percent and 9 percent of the total mortality, respectively.

- Average annual mortality was found to be just under 1 percent. The rate of mortality is about one-third higher in eastern Oregon than western Oregon.

- In eastern Oregon, about one-third of all mortality was attributed to bark beetles.

- In western Oregon, about 12 percent of mortality was attributed to root disease.

- Mortality from bark beetles was lower on private lands than on public lands. Forest Service lands are estimated to have 55 percent of the state's conifers but 83 percent of the beetle-caused mortality.

- About 16 percent, or 4,765,662 acres, of the state's forest land was found to be associated with root disease.

- Conifers were found to have higher mortality rates from bark beetles when root disease is present than when it is not.

- Conifers with moderate to severe dwarf mistletoe infections were found to have higher mortality rates than conifers without mistletoe infections.

Contents

Introduction

Forest Health

The obvious reason for quantifying insect and disease impacts in forest lands is their affect on forest health. Less obvious, is what actually constitutes forest health. Campbell and Liegel (1996) found two themes that were common in most definitions of forest health:

- A healthy forest maintains its function, diversity, and resiliency.
- A healthy forest provides for human needs and desires, and looks the way that people want it to look.

The native insects, diseases, parasites, and animals that damage and kill trees in Oregon's forests are natural parts of their ecosystems and are as responsible for creating our current forests as they are for destroying them. Tree damaging agents, by weakening and killing trees, promote the natural succession that allows new trees and forests to establish and grow. This process operates on a range of spatial and temporal scales. Endemic populations of damaging organisms may cause the slow decline and death of isolated trees, or, when conditions are right, they can rapidly increase to cause the death of an entire stand in a few years.

Insect and disease impacts that are so far outside their normal range of effects that the normal processes of recovery are diminished, or impacts that are so severe and extensive that people find them unacceptable, can be considered "unhealthy" Campbell and Liegel (1996). Several factors can predispose forests to unhealthy insect and disease events. Fire suppression and harvesting can cause unusual tree densities and species compositions to increase with time (Bergoffen 1976). When forest conditions are outside their normal range of variation, the behavior of insects, diseases, parasites, and animals may also depart from normal ranges. Introduction of nonnative damaging agents can have unpredictable effects because there may be no effective natural controls on their expansion.

Current Status, Oregon Forest Facts

Oregon forest overview—
Oregon is slightly over 61 million acres in size. Almost half of that area is currently forested. Of the forested area, 59 percent is managed by either the Forest Service or Bureau of Land Management (BLM), 21 percent is owned by forest industry, 16 percent is owned by nonindustrial private owners, and 5 percent is owned by other public agencies (Campbell et al. 2004). Of Oregon's forested area, 83 percent or 25

Almost half of Oregon's 61 million acres is forested.

million acres is in conifer forest types. The Douglas-fir forest type is the most abundant type in the state; its 11 million acres make up 37 percent of the state's forest area (table 1).

Statewide, gross annual growth of forest trees exceeds average annual mortality for all ownerships. Also, within all forest types, growth exceeds mortality. Statewide, for all owners, the growth-to-mortality ratio is 4.2 to 1. On private lands, the ratio is 6.5 to 1. On public land, the ratio is 3.3 to 1 (table 2). The difference in these ratios reflects the greater proportion of higher elevation and lower productivity forest types on public lands. When removals from harvesting are combined with mortality, growth still exceeds losses overall, but private ownerships show a net loss of volume. In western Oregon, growth exceeds mortality and removals. In eastern Oregon, growth does not match mortality and removals (table 3). To show current forest status in Oregon, the three tables on pages 3 through 7 are adapted from (Campbell et al. 2004). Those seeking more detailed information about current forest conditions should refer to Campbell et al. (2004, 2003, 2002).

Methods

Methods and Inventory Procedures

The tables 1 through 3 section from Campbell et al. (2004) were developed without the restriction of using plots that were measured at two points in time. Growth in these tables is modeled, not based on tracking individual trees through time. Mortality is calculated in these tables by applying a modeled mortality proportion to all live trees rather than subtracting trees that were thought to have died. These methods allow estimates of mortality to be made for small samples where the natural variability of mortality would make estimates vary wildly. Despite these advantages, the methods used in Campbell do not allow investigating the relationships between specific damaging agents and individual tree mortality. For this reason, the remainder of this report will use only forest inventory plots measured at two points in time.

The information used to prepare this report comes from both forest inventory plots and annual insect and disease aerial surveys. The inventory plots are maintained and measured by the Natural Resource Inventory program of the U.S. Forest Service and the BLM, and by the Forest Inventory and Analysis (FIA) Program of the Forest Service. The annual aerial surveys are a cooperative program between the Oregon Department of Forestry and the Forest Service.

Table 1—Area of forest land by forest type and owner, 1999

Forest type	All owners	All private owners	Forest industry	Native American	Other private	All public owners	Bureau of Land Management	County-municipal	National forests	Other federal	State
						Thousand acres					
Softwoods:											
Douglas-fir	11,319	4,504	3,172	168	1,164	6,815	1,581	68	4,588	5	572
Engelmann spruce	206	34	17	8	9	172		4	168		
Grand fir	1,104	169	106	25	39	935	1	7	919		8
Incense-cedar	152	103	57	8	39	49	13		36		
Jeffrey pine	38	2			2	36	7		29		
Knobcone pine	16					16			16		
Lodgepole pine	1,654	397	286	16	95	1,257	30	14	1,131	62	20
Mountain hemlock	585	32		32		553			494	59	
Noble fir	105	18	18			87		6	81		
Pacific silver fir	243	16	16			227			227		
Ponderosa pine	4,797	1,438	784	124	530	3,358	109	5	3,194		50
Port-Orford-cedar	50	19	8		11	31	8		21		2
Redwood	2	2	2								
Scotch pine	2	2			2						
Shasta red fir	188					188	7		155	27	
Sitka spruce	146	97	56		41	49		4	22		23
Subalpine fir	203					203			203		
Sugar pine	51					51	7		44		
Western hemlock	764	402	360	10	31	363	83		234		46
Western juniper	2,347	1,293	118	20	1,156	1,054	823	38	152		41
Western larch	178	30	21	2	8	148			148		
Western redcedar	107	52	24		28	55	7	3	44		
Western white pine	67					67			67		
White fir	864	258	231		27	606	57		549		
Whitebark pine	31					31			31		
All softwoods	25,221	8,870	5,275	414	3,181	16,351	2,734	149	12,552	153	763

Table 1—Area of forest land by forest type and owner, 1999 (Continued)

Forest type	All owners	All private owners	Forest industry	Native American	Other private	All public owners	Bureau of Land Management	County-municipal	National forests	Other federal	State
						Thousand acres					
Hardwoods:											
Apple	4	4	2		2						
Bigleaf maple	224	153	55		98	72	19	13	23		16
Black cottonwood	38	22	11		11	16		0	5	4	6
California black oak	103	63	20		43	40	35		5		
California-laurel	27	19	19		0	8			8		
Canyon live oak	124	41	41			83	25		58		
Chaparral	6	6	3		3						
Cherry	16	3			3	13			12		1
Golden chinkapin	60	5	5			55	20		34		
Oregon ash	32	32	6		26						
Oregon white oak	537	446	64	14	368	91	50	11	9		21
Pacific madrone	458	238	81		157	219	150	27	35		8
Quaking aspen	38	23	8		15	15			15		
Red alder	949	581	309	8	264	368	113	10	99	5	141
Tanoak	345	131	112		19	214	68		146		
White alder	5					5				5	
Willow	28	17	2		15	11			2	9	
Nonstocked	1,845	320	147	8	166	1,525	106	1	1,410	2	6
Not assessed	172	136	60	8	68	35	23		2	11	
All hardwoods	2,995	1,785	740	21	1,024	1,210	481	61	452	23	194
All forest types	30,233	11,112	6,222	452	4,439	19,122	3,344	210	14,417	189	962

Source: Campbell et al. 2004

4

Table 2—Gross annual growth and average annual mortality of growing stock trees ≥5 inches diameter at breast height on nonreserved timberland, by forest type and owner, 1999

Forest type	All owners		Private owners		Public owners	
	Current gross annual growth	Average annual mortality	Current gross annual growth	Average annual mortality	Current gross annual growth	Average annual mortality
	Thousand cubic feet					
Softwoods:						
Douglas-fir	1,304,880	242,731	555,513	61,623	749,365	181,109
Engelmann spruce	11,586	7,874	2,404	1,549	9,182	6,325
Grand fir	58,645	41,737	13,079	4,034	45,567	37,702
Incense-cedar	8,404	1,441	6,429	784	1,975	657
Jeffrey pine	705	225	39	1	666	224
Knobcone pine	722	199			722	199
Lodgepole pine	41,192	18,759	8,455	5,838	32,737	12,921
Mountain hemlock	10,901	9,356	941	2,058	9,960	7,298
Noble fir	8,404	2,649	1,047	10	7,357	2,639
Pacific silver fir	10,011	4,894	528	6	9,483	4,888
Ponderosa pine	181,198	63,877	48,660	14,022	132,539	49,856
Port-Orford-cedar	3,068	504	1,568	92	1,500	412
Redwood	1,038	302	1,038	302		
Shasta red fir	9,631	5,137			9,631	5,137
Sitka spruce	25,505	4,092	19,428	3,626	6,078	466
Subalpine fir	4,228	3,282			4,228	3,282
Sugar pine	2,200	775			2,200	775
Western hemlock	137,350	23,995	88,390	10,678	48,960	13,318
Western juniper	640	221	177	68	462	153
Western larch	7,053	5,337	1,507	816	5,546	4,521
Western redcedar	12,113	3,580	7,397	1,575	4,716	2,005
Western white pine	950	476			950	476
White fir	55,561	30,963	10,106	4,839	45,454	26,124
Whitebark pine	200	114			200	114
All softwoods	1,896,180	472,522	766,705	111,920	1,129,480	360,601

Table 2—Gross annual growth and average annual mortality of growing stock trees ≥5 inches diameter at breast height on nonreserved timberland, by forest type and owner, 1999 (continued)

Forest type	All owners		Private owners		Public owners	
	Current gross annual growth	Average annual mortality	Current gross annual growth	Average annual mortality	Current gross annual growth	Average annual mortality
	Thousand cubic feet					
Hardwoods:						
Apple	228	13	228	13		
Bigleaf maple	20,836	3,582	14,228	2,505	6,608	1,077
Black cottonwood	1,488	272	872	104	616	168
California black oak	5,237	881	2,400	603	2,837	278
California-laurel	4,648	652	3,940	561	708	91
Canyon live oak	4,467	468	569	83	3,899	385
Cherry	582	53	148	9	434	44
Golden chinkapin	4,928	513			4,928	513
Oregon ash	566	127	566	127		
Oregon white oak	12,893	2,697	10,020	2,312	2,873	386
Pacific madrone	37,894	5,670	12,479	3,021	25,416	2,649
Quaking aspen	837	236	533	123	304	113
Red alder	144,961	26,093	84,812	17,265	60,149	8,828
Tanoak	39,501	3,752	13,339	1,376	26,162	2,376
Willow	298	17	280	4	18	13
Nonstocked	12,262	3,996	2,886	854	9,377	3,142
Not assessed	15,429	1,846	15,429	1,846		
All hardwoods	279,363	45,027	144,413	28,106	134,950	16,921
All forest types	2,203,230	523,390	929,433	142,726	1,273,800	380,664

Source: Campbell et al. 2004

Table 3—Sawtimber growing-stock gross annual growth, average annual mortality, and average annual removals, by owner 1999

Owner Group	Current gross annual growth	Average annual mortality	Average annual removals
	Thousand cubic feet		
All Oregon:			
Bureau of Land Management	217,119	28,884	67,542
County-municipal	6,793	1,587	7,188
National forests	635,117	283,709	204,609
Other federal	298	59	
State	127,225	17,574	30,989
All public owners	986,552	331,812	310,329
Forest industry	518,801	66,936	580,194
Native American	12,650	10,080	18,054
Other private	171,125	35,551	135,994
All private owners	702,575	112,567	734,241
All owners	1,689,130	444,378	1,044,570
Eastern Oregon:			
Bureau of Land Management	4,705	2,941	5,228
County-municipal	153	85	133
National forests	234,209	142,493	113,855
Other federal	1	4	
State	4,547	1,678	916
All public owners	243,615	147,202	120,132
Forest industry	40,655	15,955	104,324
Other private	36,910	20,769	46,467
All private owners	77,565	36,724	150,791
All owners	321,180	183,926	270,923
Western Oregon:			
Bureau of Land Management	212,414	25,942	62,314
County-municipal	6,640	1,502	7,055
National forests	400,908	141,216	90,755
Other federal	297	55	
State	122,678	15,896	30,073
All public owners	742,937	184,610	190,197
Forest industry	478,146	50,981	475,869
Other private	146,864	24,862	107,580
All private owners	625,010	75,842	583,449
All owners	1,367,950	260,452	773,647

Source: Campbell et al. 2004

On Oregon lands administered by the Forest Service or the BLM in counties west of the Cascade crest, forest inventory plots were established using the Current Vegetation Survey (CVS) procedures (Johnson 1998, 2001). On land outside of these areas, inventory plots were installed using the procedures of the FIA Program. Both the FIA and CVS plots have been measured at two points in time approximately 10 years apart. The FIA plot data used in this study were most recently collected between 1995 and 1999 and were previously collected between 1984 and 1987. The CVS data were first collected between 1993 and 1997 and the plots were remeasured between 1997 and 2003. A minimum of 2 years and a maximum of 13 years had elapsed between the measurement of plots. More than three-quarters of the plots were measured between 6 and 12 years apart. Of the plots used for this report, 308 plots were from the BLM CVS inventory, 3,921 plots from the Forest Service CVS inventory, and 1,403 plots from the FIA inventory. To increase the precision of estimates, the BLM CVS plots were stratified by county, the Forest Service CVS plots were stratified by specific national forest and sampling intensity, and the FIA plots were stratified by using a grid of photointerpreted points as a double sample for stratification (Cochran 1977). Site classification attributes such as forest type and land use were obtained for all plots from the PNW-FIA Integrated Database (Waddell and Hiserote 2005).

On national forest land outside of designated wilderness, the CVS plots are arranged on a grid with 1.7-mile spacing. Within national forest wilderness and on BLM land in western Oregon, the plots have a 3.4-mile spacing. The CVS inventory on national forest is divided into four panels (A, B, C, and D) each containing about one-fourth of the plots. All the plots in wilderness are included in panel A. When first installed, the CVS sample design used a 185.1-foot-radius plot containing five clusters of smaller circular plots. Each of the five clusters consisted of 51.1-, 26.3-, and 11.8-foot-radius subplots. As these plots are remeasured, the 26.3-foot-radius subplot is replaced with a 24-foot-radius subplot (Johnson 2001). Unfortunately, panel C plots were remeasured before a coding system was introduced to indicate whether a tree that was present at the first measurement but was missing from the second was missing because of the change in subplot size or mortality. For this reason, panel C plots were not used in preparing this report. Only a portion of the panel B plots had been completed at the time this report was prepared.

The FIA plots are similar in layout to CVS plots, consisting of a cluster of five subplots within a 6.2-acre circle. Instead of using fixed-radii plots to sample trees, FIA plots used variable-radius (prism) plots to sample trees greater than 5 inches diameter at breast height (d.b.h.) In eastern Oregon, either a 20- or 30-foot basal area factor prism was used with a maximum sampling distance of 55.7 feet (USDA FS 1998). In western Oregon, a 7-meter basal area factor prism was used with a maximum sampling distance of 55.8 feet (USDA FS 1995).

On both the FIA and CVS plots, inventory crews sampled live and dead trees, characterized understory vegetation, and assessed site productivity and topography. Each live tree tallied on a plot was assessed for presence and severity of damaging insects, diseases, and dwarf mistletoe (*Arceuthobium* sp.).

For many pests it is appropriate to discuss their distributions according to eco-logical regions. For this report, I have used Bailey's ecoregion classification system (Bailey 2004) (fig. 1). Because the ecosection names "Willamette Valley and Puget Trough section" and "Oregon and Washington Coast Ranges section" make refer-ence to areas outside the state, I have shortened their names to "Willamette Valley section" and "Oregon Coast Ranges section" for use in this report.

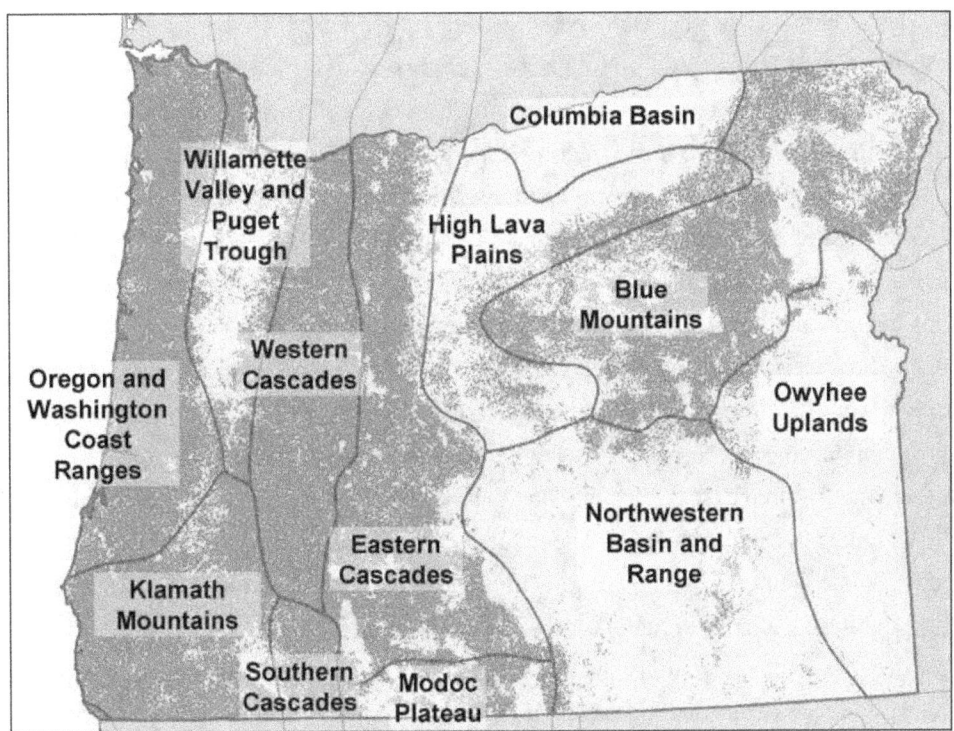

Figure 1—Bailey's Ecosections (Bailey 2004).

Reliability of Inventory Data

Estimates presented in tables in this report are accompanied by calculated standard errors. Standard errors quantify variability that was encountered during sampling. There is 68 percent confidence that an estimate presented in a table is within one standard error of the actual value. The size of the standard error in relation to the estimated value will vary with the sample size and the variability of the population sampled. In general, as a sample is divided into smaller units, the size of the standard error as a proportion of the estimate will increase. The standard errors presented in this report were calculated using an estimation program developed by Kuegler (2005) using procedures described by Bechtold and Patterson (2005).

Causes of Damage and Mortality

Overall, 36 percent of the live trees sampled had at least one kind of injury recorded (table 4). The most common damages recorded were physical injuries such as dead tops, basal scars, and forks. It is likely that many of the trees recorded with physical damage had been damaged previously by an insect, disease, animal, or weather event, but it could no longer be specifically identified by the time the trees were assessed. The types of damage commonly recorded varied across the state. In the wetter forests of western Oregon, 26 percent of the trees had damage, with root diseases being the most prevalent agent aside from physical damage. In the drier forests east of the Cascade crest, damage was about twice as common. About the same proportion of trees had root disease as in the west but mistletoes, bark beetles, defoliators, and cankers were much more prevalent in the east.

> **In the wetter forests of western Oregon, 26 percent of the trees had damage; in the drier forests east of the Cascade crest, damage was about twice as common.**

Where trees were found to have died between plot measurements, inventory crews would attempt to identify the cause of mortality. Because of the time interval between plot measurements, it was not always possible to identify the agent of mortality. In some cases, trees that had died may have been salvaged before inventory crews returned to the plot. The evidence of some agents, such as defoliating insects, is ephemeral in nature and is not likely to be identified more than a year or two after death. Other agents, such as root rots may leave evidence that persists for decades. Not surprisingly, the most commonly recorded causes of death were "unknown" and "physical damage." It is likely that many of the trees with mortality attributed to physical damage were killed by other agents and had fallen or broken by the time they were remeasured by inventory crews. Both categories would also include trees that had died through suppression, a process where a tree dies from receiving inadequate sunlight owing to crowding and shading by other trees. The

Table 4—Number and proportion of live trees ≥5 inches diameter at breast height with damage, by damage type and region of state, 1995–2003

Damage type	All Oregon				Western Oregon				Eastern Oregon			
	Total	SE	Proportion	SE	Total	SE	Proportion	SE	Total	SE	Proportion	SE
	Million trees		*Percent*		*Million trees*		*Percent*		*Million trees*		*Percent*	
Root disease	228	12	6.0	0.3	137	9	5.6	0.4	91	7	6.7	0.5
Bark beetles	50	3	1.3	0.1	6	1	0.3	0.1	44	2	3.2	0.1
Mistletoe	290	12	7.6	0.3	80	7	3.3	0.3	210	9	15.4	0.6
Defoliators	100	9	2.6	0.2	21	5	0.8	0.2	80	8	5.8	0.6
Other insects	8	1	0.2	<0.1	5	1	0.2	<0.1	3	1	0.2	0.1
Cankers	109	5	2.9	0.1	34	3	1.4	0.1	75	4	5.4	0.3
Stem decays	119	5	3.1	0.1	87	5	3.6	0.2	32	1	2.3	0.1
Foliar pathogens	19	2	0.5	0.1	8	2	0.3	0.1	11	2	0.8	0.1
Animals	24	2	0.6	<0.1	8	1	0.3	<0.1	16	2	1.2	0.1
Weather	27	2	0.7	0.1	16	2	0.7	0.1	11	1	0.8	0.1
Physical damage	780	15	20.5	0.3	359	12	14.8	0.4	421	9	30.7	0.5
Any damage	1,368	23	36.0	0.5	629	17	25.9	0.6	739	16	54.0	0.7
All trees	3,801	47			2,432	41			1,369	23		

Data do not total because trees often have more than one type of damage.

SE = standard error.

Most tree species had less than 2 percent annual mortality.

next most commonly recorded causes of mortality were bark beetles and root diseases with 19 and 9 percent of the total mortality, respectively. As with agents recorded on live trees, the causes of mortality are not uniform across the state. Nearly twice as much mortality is attributed to root disease in western Oregon as in eastern Oregon. In western Oregon, about 4 percent of total mortality was attributed to bark beetles whereas in eastern Oregon, about one-third of all mortality was attributed to bark beetles (table 5). There was also variation in mortality rates by tree species. Most tree species had less than 2 percent annual mortality. Douglas-fir (see "Names of Trees" for scientific names) had a mortality rate of less than 1 percent per year, and subalpine fir was found to have an annual mortality rate of 3.7 percent (table 6).

The trees that died between plot measurements represent an annual volume loss of about 2.4 billion board feet across the state. The proportion of mortality volume attributed to each cause of death is similar to the proportion of trees killed by each cause of death except that physical damages and unknown causes each account for about 30 percent of the volume lost. Physical damages, unknown damages, and bark beetles together account for over 70 percent of the mortality volume (table 7). The overall average annual mortality amounts to 0.6 percent of the gross board foot volume of live trees. The rate of annual mortality of volume differs across the state. Although eastern Oregon has about one-third of the state's total live volume, almost half of the state's mortality was found in the east. Eastern Oregon's 1.1 percent estimated rate of annual mortality of volume is more than double the estimated rate for western Oregon (table 8).

Insects

Bark beetles—

Of all insects damaging trees in Oregon, bark beetles were designated as the cause of mortality about six times as often as defoliators and other insects. Bark beetles burrow into the bark of trees and lay their eggs underneath. The maturing larvae then feed on the tree's cambium (fig. 2.) Trees are often killed by the severing of their conductive tissues either directly by larval feeding or by stain fungi introduced by the beetles. Twenty-two percent of the conifer mortality volume detected on plots was attributed to bark beetles. For Engelmann spruce, grand fir, lodgepole pine, ponderosa pine, subalpine fir, and western larch close to, or more than a third of total mortality was attributed to bark beetles (table 9). At low endemic population levels, bark beetles typically attack and feed on trees that are stressed by competition, drought, other insects, or diseases. Trees of low vigor are more susceptible

Table 5—Average annual mortality and proportion of total mortality by cause of death, trees ≥5 inches diameter at breast height, 1984–2003

Cause of death	All Oregon				Western Oregon				Eastern Oregon			
	Total	SE	Proportion	SE	Total	SE	Proportion	SE	Total	SE	Proportion	SE
	Thousand trees		*Percent*		*Thousand trees*		*Percent*		*Thousand trees*		*Percent*	
Root disease	2,946	278	8.6	0.8	1,997	250	11.5	1.3	949	123	5.6	0.7
Bark beetles	6,462	442	18.9	1.2	719	167	4.1	0.9	5,744	410	34.2	1.9
Mistletoe	384	59	1.1	0.2	201	47	1.2	0.3	183	36	1.1	0.2
Defoliators	740	150	2.2	0.4	94	38	0.5	0.2	646	145	3.8	0.9
Other insects	256	76	0.7	0.2	113	28	0.6	0.2	143	71	0.9	0.4
Cankers	354	58	1.3	0.2	92	27	1.0	0.2	262	51	1.6	0.3
Stem decays	844	129	2.5	0.4	641	125	3.7	0.7	203	34	1.2	0.2
Foliar pathogens	31	19	0.1	0.1	27	19	0.2	0.1	4	4	0	<0.1
Animals	126	41	0.4	0.1	117	40	0.7	0.2	9	5	0.1	<0.1
Weather	1,458	262	4.3	0.7	1,249	257	7.2	1.4	209	51	1.2	0.3
Physical damage	8,399	555	24.6	1.3	4,250	374	24.4	1.8	4,149	410	24.7	1.9
Unknown cause	12,211	578	35.4	1.3	7,911	523	45	2.0	4,300	249	25.5	1.3
All causes	34,212	1,125	100		17,411	850	100		16,801	741	100	

SE = standard error.

Table 6—Number of live trees ≥5 inches diameter at breast height, average annual mortality, and proportion of live trees killed annualy, by species and region, 1984–2003

Tree species	Live		Annual mortality			
	Total	SE	Total	SE	Proprotion	SE
	– – Thousand trees – –		– – – – – – – Percent – – – – – – –			
All Oregon:						
Douglas-fir	1,218,263	29,117	7,858	522	0.6	<0.1
Engelmann spruce	26,697	2,387	538	115	2.0	0.4
Grand fir	173,130	8,637	2,529	263	1.5	0.1
Lodgepole pine	296,193	13,732	4,497	359	1.5	0.1
Mountain hemlock	133,029	10,038	1,433	303	1.1	0.2
Noble fir	21,726	4,137	284	93	1.3	0.4
Pacific silver fir	89,615	7,962	1,375	175	1.5	0.2
Ponderosa pine	454,747	13,500	3,255	294	0.7	0.1
Shasta red fir	23,439	3,504	194	53	0.8	0.2
Sitka spruce	20,727	4,411	104	40	0.5	0.2
Subalpine fir	55,181	5,433	2,048	281	3.7	0.4
Sugar pine	11,084	1,262	183	55	1.7	0.4
Western hemlock	286,270	20,164	1,903	285	0.7	0.1
Western larch	34,485	3,339	333	55	1.0	0.1
White fir	174,756	10,612	1,828	232	1.0	0.1
Other pines	29,705	3,100	407	55	1.4	0.2
Other conifers	144,257	7,407	661	149	0.5	0.1
All conifers	3,193,304	42,756	29,428	1,030	0.9	<0.1
All hardwoods	595,348	23,542	4,784	427	0.8	0.1
All trees	3,788,652	48,106	34,212	1,125	0.9	<0.1
Eastern Oregon:						
Douglas-fir	189,254	8,987	1,947	205	1.0	0.1
Engelmann spruce	25,108	2,346	504	115	2.0	0.4
Grand fir	140,710	7,424	2,096	238	1.5	0.1
Lodgepole pine	266,901	13,035	4,125	350	1.5	0.1
Mountain hemlock	60,124	6,821	593	173	1.0	0.3
Noble fir	4,760	1,948	102	68	2.1	1.3
Pacific silver fir	11,637	2,516	219	75	1.9	0.6
Ponderosa pine	434,360	13,126	3,184	293	0.7	0.1
Shasta red fir	14,104	2,493	148	48	1.1	0.2
Sitka spruce						
Subalpine fir	45,259	4,911	1,463	204	3.2	0.4
Sugar pine	2,700	558	12	7	0.4	0.2
Western hemlock	3,324	1,325	5	2	0.2	0.1
Western larch	34,214	3,337	332	55	1.0	0.1
White fir	121,057	9,512	1,593	228	1.3	0.2
Other pines	11,324	1,429	227	41	2.0	0.3
Other conifers	42,384	3,020	138	35	0.3	0.1
All conifers	1,407,221	23,260	16,688	741	1.2	<0.1
All hardwoods	7,478	1,977	113	36	1.5	0.4
All trees	1,414,699	23,362	16,801	741	1.2	<0.1

Table 6—Number of live trees ≥5 inches diameter at breast height, average annual mortality, and proportion of live trees killed annualy, by species and region, 1984–2003 (continued)

Tree species	Live		Annual mortality			
	Total	SE	Total	SE	Proprotion	SE
	– – Thousand trees – –		– – – – – – – – Percent – – – – – – – –			
Western Oregon:						
Douglas-fir	1,029,009	27,735	5,911	481	0.6	<0.1
Engelmann spruce	1,589	442	34	12	2.1	0.6
Grand fir	32,420	4,435	433	112	1.3	0.3
Lodgepole pine	29,291	4,322	372	81	1.3	0.2
Mountain hemlock	72,905	7,453	840	249	1.2	0.3
Noble fir	16,966	3,655	182	64	1.1	0.3
Pacific silver fir	77,978	7,572	1,155	158	1.5	0.2
Ponderosa pine	20,387	3,154	71	24	0.3	0.1
Shasta red fir	9,335	2,469	46	22	0.5	0.2
Sitka spruce	20,727	4,411	104	40	0.5	0.2
Subalpine fir	9,921	2,323	585	193	5.9	1.1
Sugar pine	8,384	1,131	171	55	2.0	0.5
Western hemlock	282,946	20,130	1,898	285	0.7	0.1
Western larch	271	117	1	0	0.2	0.2
White fir	53,699	4,727	234	43	0.4	0.1
Other pines	18,381	2,751	180	37	1.0	0.2
Other conifers	101,873	6,766	522	145	0.5	0.1
All conifers	1,786,082	36,327	12,740	720	0.7	<0.1
All hardwoods	587,871	23,460	4,671	425	0.8	0.1
All trees	2,373,953	42,468	17,411	850	0.7	<0.1

SE = standard error.

Table 7—Average annual mortality volume and proportion of mortality volume, by cause of death, conifers ≥9 inches and hardwoods ≥11 inches diameter at breast height, 1984–2003

Cause of death	All Oregon				Western Oregon				Eastern Oregon			
	Total	SE	Proportion	SE	Total	SE	Proportion	SE	Total	SE	Proportion	SE
	Million board feet		*Percent*		*Million board feet*		*Percent*		*Million board feet*		*Percent*	
Root disease	213	19	8.7	0.8	122	14	9.5	1.1	91	13	7.8	1.1
Bark beetles	541	41	22.1	1.5	124	22	9.6	1.6	417	34	36.0	2.6
Mistletoe	39	7	1.6	0.3	24	6	1.8	0.4	16	4	1.4	0.3
Defoliators	20	5	0.8	0.2	2	1	0.2	0.1	17	5	1.5	0.4
Other insects	11	3	0.5	0.1	7	2	0.5	0.2	4	2	0.4	0.2
Cankers	12	3	0.5	0.1	8	2	0.6	0.2	4	1	0.3	0.1
Stem decays	131	17	5.4	0.7	87	15	6.8	1.1	44	7	3.8	0.6
Foliar pathogens	2	2	0.1	0.1	1	1	0.1	0.1	1	1	0.1	0.1
Animals	3	1	0.1	0	2	1	0.2	0.1	0	0	0	0
Weather	68	15	2.8	0.6	53	15	4.1	1.1	15	4	1.3	0.3
Physical damage	751	60	30.7	1.8	416	41	32.2	2.4	335	44	28.9	2.7
Unknown cause	658	51	26.9	1.6	445	46	34.4	2.6	214	22	18.4	1.5
All causes	2,448	109	100		1,291	81	100		1,158	73	100	

SE = standard error.

Table 8—Volume of live trees and average annual mortality volume, (conifers ≥9 inches and hardwoods ≥11 inches diameter at breast height), by species and region, 1984–2003

| Tree species | Live | | Annual mortality | | | |
	Total	SE	Total	SE	Proportion of live	SE
	– – – – – – *Million board feet* – – – – – –				– – – *Percent* – – –	
All Oregon:						
Douglas-fir	219,815	5,276	791	59	0.4	0
Engelmann spruce	4,310	503	80	20	1.9	0.4
Grand fir	17,351	1,015	240	23	1.4	0.1
Lodgepole pine	7,019	398	99	9	1.4	0.1
Mountain hemlock	13,362	1,283	159	49	1.2	0.3
Noble fir	4,984	755	62	29	1.2	0.5
Pacific silver fir	6,625	680	78	12	1.2	0.2
Ponderosa pine	37,771	1,018	203	21	0.5	0.1
Shasta red fir	5,151	842	30	9	0.6	0.1
Sitka spruce	5,498	1,579	10	5	0.2	0.1
Subalpine fir	1,921	221	70	10	3.6	0.4
Sugar pine	4,442	485	31	10	0.7	0.2
Western hemlock	31,063	1,839	174	24	0.6	0.1
Western larch	4,324	355	42	8	1.0	0.2
White fir	16,068	1,051	188	24	1.2	0.1
Other pines	2,584	215	49	11	1.9	0.4
Other conifers	12,802	860	26	4	0.2	0
All conifers	395,089	6,638	2,333	109	0.6	0
All hardwoods	20,334	1,068	115	13	0.6	0.1
All trees	415,423	6,764	2,448	109	0.6	0
Eastern Oregon:						
Douglas-fir	17,081	825	154	18	0.9	0.1
Engelmann spruce	3,924	488	75	20	1.9	0.4
Grand fir	13,645	875	209	22	1.5	0.1
Lodgepole pine	6,169	372	88	8	1.4	0.1
Mountain hemlock	7,381	1,064	81	33	1.1	0.4
Noble fir	637	277	29	27	4.6	2.6
Pacific silver fir	768	184	19	8	2.5	0.9
Ponderosa pine	35,173	971	196	20	0.6	0.1
Shasta red fir	3,174	714	18	6	0.6	0.1
Sitka spruce					0	0
Subalpine fir	1,681	210	58	9	3.4	0.4
Sugar pine	331	71	0	0	0.1	0.1
Western hemlock	541	208	2	1	0.3	0.2
Western larch	4,198	348	40	8	1.0	0.2
White fir	9,402	824	157	23	1.7	0.2
Other pines	1,047	128	25	6	2.3	0.5
Other conifers	1,130	186	3	1	0.3	0.1
All conifers	106,282	2,326	1,154	73	1.1	0.1
All hardwoods	266	113	3	1	1.3	0.6
All trees	106,548	2,331	1,158	73	1.1	0.1

Table 8—Volume of live trees and average annual mortality volume, (conifers ≥9 inches and hardwoods ≥11 inches diameter at breast height), by species and region, 1984–2003 (continued)

Tree species	Live		Annual mortality			
	Total	SE	Total	SE	Proportion of live	SE
	– – – – – – Million board feet – – – – – –				– – – Percent – – –	
Western Oregon:						
Douglas-fir	202,734	5,223	637	56	0.3	0
Engelmann spruce	386	124	6	3	1.5	0.3
Grand fir	3,705	515	32	7	0.9	0.2
Lodgepole pine	850	141	10	2	1.2	0.2
Mountain hemlock	5,981	719	78	36	1.3	0.6
Noble fir	4,347	703	33	11	0.8	0.2
Pacific silver fir	5,857	656	59	9	1.0	0.1
Ponderosa pine	2,597	307	7	5	0.3	0.2
Shasta red fir	1,977	449	12	7	0.6	0.3
Sitka spruce	5,498	1,579	10	5	0.2	0.1
Subalpine fir	240	71	12	5	5.1	1.1
Sugar pine	4,111	479	31	10	0.7	0.2
Western hemlock	30,522	1,833	172	24	0.6	0.1
Western larch	126	72	1	1	0.9	0.5
White fir	6,665	657	31	6	0.5	0.1
Other pines	1,537	172	25	9	1.6	0.6
Other conifers	11,673	840	23	4	0.2	0
All conifers	288,807	6,277	1,179	81	0.4	0
All hardwoods	20,068	1,062	112	13	0.6	0.1
All trees	308,874	6,410	1,291	81	0.4	0

SE = standard error.

Ladd Livingston, Idaho Department of Lands, Bugwood.org.

Figure 2—Mountain pine beetle galleries on wood surface.

Table 9—Average annual conifer mortality and mortality from bark beetles (trees ≥5 inches diameter at breast height), by species and region 1984–2003

Tree species	Annual mortality	SE	Annual mortality from bark beetles	SE	Annual proportion killed by bark beetles	SE
	------ Thousand trees -------				-- Percent --	
All Oregon:						
Douglas-fir	7,858	522	923	165	11.7	2.0
Engelmann spruce	538	115	244	96	45.4	9.6
Grand fir	2,529	263	1,038	185	41.0	5.0
Lodgepole pine	4,497	359	1,444	181	32.1	2.8
Mountain hemlock	1,433	303	42	12	2.9	1.0
Noble fir	284	93	5	5	1.8	1.9
Pacific silver fir	1,375	175	122	31	8.9	2.0
Ponderosa pine	3,255	294	1,191	144	36.6	3.8
Shasta red fir	194	53	36	17	18.5	6.5
Sitka spruce	104	40				
Subalpine fir	2,048	281	665	121	32.5	4.4
Sugar pine	183	55	27	11	14.7	6.8
Western hemlock	1,903	285	16	10	0.8	0.5
Western larch	333	55	143	31	42.9	6.2
White fir	1,828	232	421	115	23.0	5.1
Other pines	407	55	121	26	29.6	5.1
Other conifers	661	149	17	10	2.6	1.6
All conifers	29,428	1,030	6,454	442	21.9	1.3
Eastern Oregon:						
Douglas-fir	1,947	205	566	70	29.1	3.5
Engelmann spruce	504	115	243	96	48.2	9.8
Grand fir	2,096	238	1,005	184	47.9	5.3
Lodgepole pine	4,125	350	1,403	178	34.0	2.9
Mountain hemlock	593	173	33	11	5.6	2.2
Noble fir	102	68				
Pacific silver fir	219	75	30	15	13.5	6.8
Ponderosa pine	3,184	293	1,184	144	37.2	3.9
Shasta red fir	148	48	34	17	22.8	8.0
Sitka spruce						
Subalpine fir	1,463	204	563	112	38.5	5.0
Sugar pine	12	7	10	6	82.9	16.1
Western hemlock	5	2				
Western larch	332	55	143	31	43.0	6.2
White fir	1,593	228	399	114	25.0	5.7
Other pines	227	41	107	25	47.1	6.3
Other conifers	138	35	17	10	12.4	7.0
All conifers	16,688	741	5,736	410	34.4	1.9

Table 9—Average annual conifer mortality and mortality from bark beetles (trees ≥5 inches diameter at breast height), by species and region 1984–2003 (continued)

Tree species	Annual mortality	SE	Annual mortality from bark beetles	SE	Annual proportion killed by bark beetles	SE
	– – – – – – – *Thousand trees* – – – – – – –				– – *Percent* – –	
Western Oregon:						
Douglas-fir	5,911	481	357	150	6.0	2.4
Engelmann spruce	34	12	1	1	2.8	2.9
Grand fir	433	112	33	16	7.7	3.8
Lodgepole pine	372	81	41	32	11.1	7.9
Mountain hemlock	840	249	8	5	1.0	0.6
Noble fir	182	64	5	5	2.8	3.0
Pacific silver fir	1,155	158	93	27	8.0	2.1
Ponderosa pine	71	24	7	7	9.9	8.5
Shasta red fir	46	22	2	1	4.3	2.6
Sitka spruce	104	40				
Subalpine fir	585	193	101	45	17.3	6.0
Sugar pine	171	55	17	9	10.1	5.7
Western hemlock	1,898	285	16	10	0.8	0.5
Western larch	1	0				
White fir	234	43	22	10	9.3	4.1
Other pines	180	37	14	7	7.6	3.9
Other conifers	522	145			0	0
All conifers	12,740	720	718	167	5.6	1.3

SE = standard error.

to attack because they are less able to "pitch out" attacking beetles than healthier trees (Goheen and Willhite 2006). Bark beetles often serve the role of thinning weaker trees from stands or killing stands of trees that have become overcrowded. Occasionally, bark beetle populations will build up to outbreak levels where their sheer numbers allow them to overwhelm natural defenses of otherwise healthy trees.

Trees are killed by bark beetles at different rates depending on tree species and region of the state. Nearly all conifer species were estimated to have higher rates of mortality from bark beetles in eastern Oregon than western (table 10). Of the 395 billion gross board feet of conifer volume in the state, an estimated 540 million board feet was killed annually by bark beetles between 1984 and 2003; nearly 70 percent of this mortality occurred in eastern Oregon (table 11). Subalpine fir was the only species found to have an annual mortality of volume from bark beetles significantly greater than 1 percent (at the 66 percent confidence level). Based on

Of the 395 billion gross board feet of conifer volume in the state, an estimated 540 million board feet was killed annually between 1984 and 2003; nearly 70 percent of this mortality occurred in eastern Oregon.

Table 10—Number of live conifers ≥5 inches diameter at breast height at first measurement and average annual conifer mortality from bark beetles, by species and region, 1984–2003

Tree species	Annual mortality	SE	Annual mortality from bark beetles	SE	Annual proportion killed by bark beetles	SE
	– – – – – – Thousand trees – – – – – –				– – Percent – –	
All Oregon:						
Douglas-fir	1,218,263	29,117	923	165	0.1	<0.1
Engelmann spruce	26,697	2,387	244	96	0.9	0.3
Grand fir	173,130	8,637	1,038	185	0.6	0.1
Lodgepole pine	296,193	13,732	1,444	181	0.5	0.1
Mountain hemlock	133,029	10,038	42	12	<0.1	<0.1
Noble fir	21,726	4,137	5	5	<0.1	<0.1
Pacific silver fir	89,615	7,962	122	31	0.1	<0.1
Ponderosa pine	454,747	13,500	1,191	144	0.3	<0.1
Shasta red fir	23,439	3,504	36	17	0.2	0.1
Sitka spruce	20,727	4,411	0			
Subalpine fir	55,181	5,433	665	121	1.2	0.2
Sugar pine	11,084	1,262	27	11	0.2	0.1
Western hemlock	286,270	20,164	16	10	<0.1	<0.1
Western larch	34,485	3,339	143	31	0.4	0.1
White fir	174,756	10,612	421	115	0.2	0.1
Other pines	29,705	3,100	121	26	0.4	0.1
Other conifers	144,257	7,407	17	10	<0.1	<0.1
All conifers	3,193,304	42,756	6,454	442	0.2	<0.1
Eastern Oregon:						
Douglas-fir	189,254	8,987	566	70	0.3	<0.1
Engelmann spruce	25,108	2,346	243	96	1	0.4
Grand fir	140,710	7,424	1,005	184	0.7	0.1
Lodgepole pine	266,901	13,035	1,403	178	0.5	0.1
Mountain hemlock	60,124	6,821	33	11	0.1	<0.1
Noble fir	4,760	1,948	<1			
Pacific silver fir	11,637	2,516	30	15	0.3	0.1
Ponderosa pine	434,360	13,126	1,184	144	0.3	<0.1
Shasta red fir	14,104	2,493	34	17	0.2	0.1
Sitka spruce	<1					
Subalpine fir	45,259	4,911	563	112	1.2	0.2
Sugar pine	2,700	558	10	6	0.4	0.2
Western hemlock	3,324	1,325	<1		<0.1	<0.1
Western larch	34,214	3,337	143	31	0.4	0.1
White fir	121,057	9,512	399	114	0.3	0.1
Other pines	11,324	1,429	107	25	0.9	0.2
Other conifers	42,384	3,020	17	10	<0.1	<0.1
All conifers	1,407,221	23,260	5,736	410	0.4	<0.1

Table 10—Number of live conifers ≥5 inches diameter at breast height at first measurement and average annual conifer mortality from bark beetles, by species and region, 1984–2003 (continued)

Tree species	Annual mortality	SE	Annual mortality from bark beetles	SE	Annual proportion killed by bark beetles	SE
	— — — — — — Thousand trees — — — — — —				— — Percent — —	
Western Oregon:						
Douglas-fir	1,029,009	27,735	357	150	<0.1	<0.1
Engelmann spruce	1,589	442	1	1	0.1	0.1
Grand fir	32,420	4,435	33	16	0.1	<0.1
Lodgepole pine	29,291	4,322	41	32	0.1	0.1
Mountain hemlock	72,905	7,453	8	5	<0.1	<0.1
Noble fir	16,966	3,655	5	5	<0.1	<0.1
Pacific silver fir	77,978	7,572	93	27	0.1	<0.1
Ponderosa pine	20,387	3,154	7	7	<0.1	<0.1
Shasta red fir	9,335	2,469	2	1	<0.1	<0.1
Sitka spruce	20,727	4,411	<1			
Subalpine fir	9,921	2,323	101	45	1	0.3
Sugar pine	8,384	1,131	17	9	0.2	0.1
Western hemlock	282,946	20,130	16	10	<0.1	<0.1
Western larch	271	117	<1			
White fir	53,699	4,727	22	10	<0.1	<0.1
Other pines	18,381	2,751	14	7	0.1	<0.1
Other conifers	101,873	6,766	<1			
All conifers	1,786,082	36,327	718	167	<0.1	<0.1

SE = standard error.

Table 11—Volume of live conifers ≥9 inches diameter at breast height at first measurement and average annual conifer mortality from bark beetles, by species and region, 1984–2003

Tree species	Annual mortality	SE	Annual mortality from bark beetles	SE	Annual proportion killed by bark beetles	SE
	------- Thousand trees -------				-- Percent --	
All Oregon:						
Douglas-fir	219,815	5,276	140	22	0.1	<0.1
Engelmann spruce	4,310	503	41	18	1	0.4
Grand fir	17,351	1,015	104	12	0.6	0.1
Lodgepole pine	7,019	398	38	5	0.5	0.1
Mountain hemlock	13,362	1,283	5	2	<0.1	<0.1
Noble fir	4,984	755	0	0	<0.1	<0.1
Pacific silver fir	6,625	680	11	3	0.2	<0.1
Ponderosa pine	37,771	1,018	73	10	0.2	<0.1
Shasta red fir	5,151	842	8	4	0.2	0.1
Sitka spruce	5,498	1,579	<1		<0.1	<0.1
Subalpine fir	1,921	221	30	6	1.6	0.2
Sugar pine	4,442	485	12	5	0.3	0.1
Western hemlock	31,063	1,839	3	2	<0.1	<0.1
Western larch	4,324	355	19	5	0.4	0.1
White fir	16,068	1,051	34	5	0.2	<0.1
Other pines	2,584	215	21	9	0.8	0.4
Other conifers	12,802	860	0	0	<0.1	<0.1
All conifers	395,089	6,638	540	41	0.1	<0.1
Eastern Oregon:						
Douglas-fir	17,081	825	68	12	0.4	0.1
Engelmann spruce	3,924	488	41	18	1	0.4
Grand fir	13,645	875	101	12	0.7	0.1
Lodgepole pine	6,169	372	36	5	0.6	0.1
Mountain hemlock	7,381	1,064	4	2	0.1	0
Noble fir	637	277	<1	<1	<0.1	<0.1
Pacific silver fir	768	184	2	1	0.3	0.1
Ponderosa pine	35,173	971	73	10	0.2	<0.1
Shasta red fir	3,174	714	3	2	0.1	0.1
Sitka spruce	<1	<1	<1	<1	<0.1	<0.1
Subalpine fir	1,681	210	28	5	1.6	0.2
Sugar pine	331	71	<1	<1	<0.1	<0.1
Western hemlock	541	208	<1	<1	<0.1	<0.1
Western larch	4,198	348	19	5	0.5	0.1
White fir	9,402	824	30	5	0.3	0.1
Other pines	1,047	128	12	5	1.1	0.4
Other conifers	1,130	186	<1	<1	<0.1	<0.1
All conifers	106,282	2,326	417	34	0.4	<0.1

Table 11—Volume of live conifers ≥9 inches diameter at breast height at first measurement and average annual conifer mortality from bark beetles, by species and region, 1984–2003 (continued)

Tree species	Annual mortality	SE	Annual mortality from bark beetles	SE	Annual proportion killed by bark beetles	SE
	------- Thousand trees -------				-- Percent --	
Western Oregon:						
Douglas-fir	202,734	5,223	72	18	<0.1	<0.1
Engelmann spruce	386	124	<1	0	<0.1	<0.1
Grand fir	3,705	515	3	2	0.1	<0.1
Lodgepole pine	850	141	2	1	0.2	0.1
Mountain hemlock	5,981	719	1	0	<0.1	<0.1
Noble fir	4,347	703	<1	0	<0.1	<0.1
Pacific silver fir	5,857	656	9	3	0.2	<0.1
Ponderosa pine	2,597	307	<1	0	<0.1	<0.1
Shasta red fir	1,977	449	5	3	0.2	0.2
Sitka spruce	5,498	1,579	<1	<1	<0.1	<0.1
Subalpine fir	240	71	2	1	1	0.5
Sugar pine	4,111	479	12	5	0.3	0.1
Western hemlock	30,522	1,833	3	2	<0.1	<0.1
Western larch	126	72	<1	<1	<0.1	<0.1
White fir	6,665	657	4	2	0.1	<0.1
Other pines	1,537	172	10	8	0.6	0.5
Other conifers	11,673	840	<1	<1	<0.1	<0.1
All conifers	288,807	6,277	124	22	<0.1	<0.1

SE = standard error.

the number of trees killed, the most important bark beetles occurring in Oregon are the fir engraver beetle *Scolytus ventralis* LeConte, the mountain pine beetle *Dendroctonus ponderosae* Hopkins, and the Douglas-fir beetle *D. pseudotsugae* Hopkins. Bark beetles are often difficult to detect in live trees until crown symptoms or pitch streams are evident. After tree death, identifying the beetle species that killed the tree can be done by examining the gallery pattern etched into the wood or bark by tunneling adults or larvae. When the beetle galleries could not be closely examined by the crews, they recorded a nonspecified beetle. Because individual bark beetle species have preferences for certain species and sizes of host trees, it is often possible to attribute mortality to specific beetle species based on the attributes of the tree that was killed.

When a specific bark beetle could be identified as killing true firs (*Abies* spp.), the identified beetle was nearly always the fir engraver beetle. It is likely that most firs recorded as beetle killed were killed by fir engraver beetles. The most recent outbreak of fir engraver beetle occurred in Lake and Klamath Counties during 1995 and 1996 (Nelson 2005).

The most important beetle attacking pines (*Pinus* spp.) in Oregon is the mountain pine beetle. The mountain pine beetle has a preference for pines between about 6 and 20 inches d.b.h., and most of the beetle-caused mortality of pines this size can be attributed to this beetle (Amman et al. 1989). The western pine beetle *Dendroctonus brevicomis* Le Conte and the pine engraver beetle *Ips pini* Say, are also important causes of mortality of ponderosa pine. The pine engraver beetle commonly attacks ponderosa pine 5 to 8 inches d.b.h. growing in crowded conditions (Kegley et al. 1997). The western pine beetle will attack trees as small as 6 inches d.b.h. and will also attack trees larger than the mountain pine beetle will (DeMars and Roettgering 1982). Most beetle-killed ponderosa pines larger than 20 inches d.b.h. are likely victims of this beetle.

Bark beetles at endemic levels may cause isolated mortality to weakened trees in otherwise healthy stands. This sort of mortality is generally not indicative of a forest health problem. When populations build up to cause appreciable levels of mortality, trees will be killed in groups that may cover many acres. Table 12 shows the acreage of forest types where bark beetles have caused greater than 25 percent mortality to conifer basal area over a decade. Figure 3 shows the distribution of this acreage over the state. Western Oregon had about 41,000 acres of forest where beetles had caused this level of mortality, with over half of these acres in the Douglas-fir forest type. However, as there are over 9 million acres of Douglas-fir type in western Oregon, this amount of mortality amounted to less than 1 percent of the Douglas-fir type. Eastern Oregon on the other hand, had about 370,000 acres (2.5 percent of the forested area) where bark beetles had killed more than 25 percent of the conifers over a decade. In eastern Oregon, the Engelmann spruce and grand fir forest types had higher than average proportions of bark-beetle-affected area (17 percent and 8 percent, respectively). Subalpine fir and western larch forest types both had relatively high estimates of area with high levels of bark beetle mortality, but sampling error is too high in these types to conclude that these levels are different than the average value for eastern Oregon. That western larch forest type has bark beetle mortality is at first surprising because the western larch is generally thought to be a poor host to bark beetles (Burns and Honkala 1990) However, it is common for stands that are predominately larch to have significant

Table 12—Total area and area where >25 percent of conifer basal area was killed by bark beetles, by forest type, and region, 1984–2003

Forest type	Area	With >25% conifer mortality from bark beetles	SE	Proportion	SE
	——————— Acres ———————			— — Percent — —	
All Oregon:					
Douglas-fir	11,494,127	77,272	17,434	0.7	0.2
Engelmann spruce	202,108	34,336	13,609	17.0	6.1
Grand fir	1,063,255	75,670	17,372	7.1	1.6
Lodgepole pine	1,638,876	60,503	16,998	3.7	1.0
Mountain hemlock	584,540	<1			
Noble fir	105,296	<1			
Pacific silver fir	289,938	<1			
Ponderosa pine	4,889,608	51,472	13,550	1.1	0.3
Shasta red fir	176,829	2,401	2,354	1.4	1.3
Sitka spruce	168,951	<1			
Subalpine fir	196,686	17,009	10,910	8.6	5.2
Western hemlock	762,160	<1			
Western larch	183,156	12,983	7,711	7.1	4.1
White fir	883,017	1,024	1,016	0.1	0.1
Other conifers	516,124	6,473	4,650	1.3	0.9
Hardwood, juniper, and nonstocked	7,036,784	72,023	19,168	1.0	0.3
All forest types	30,191,457	411,165	42,177	1.4	0.1
Eastern Oregon:					
Douglas-fir	1,731,919	53,610	14,693	3.1	0.8
Engelmann spruce	200,564	34,336	13,609	17.1	6.1
Grand fir	998,850	75,670	17,372	7.6	1.7
Lodgepole pine	1,540,146	56,749	16,568	3.7	1.1
Mountain hemlock	282,393	<1			
Noble fir	20,234	<1			
Pacific silver fir	25,700	<1			
Ponderosa pine	4,797,208	51,472	13,550	1.1	0.3
Shasta red fir	122,780	2,401	2,354	2.0	1.9
Sitka spruce	0	0			
Subalpine fir	172,643	17,009	10,910	9.9	5.9
Western hemlock	22,886	<1			
Western larch	183,156	12,983	7,711	7.1	4.1
White fir	627,106	1,024	1,016	0.2	0.2
Other conifers	93,456	6,473	4,650	6.9	4.9
Hardwood, juniper, and nonstocked	4,272,577	58,041	15,075	1.4	0.4
All forest types	15,091,616	369,767	39,195	2.5	0.3

Table 12—Total area and area where >25 percent of conifer basal area was killed by bark beetles, by forest type, and region, 1984–2003 (continued)

Forest type	Area	With >25% conifer mortality from bark beetles	SE	Proportion	SE
		— — — — — — — Acres — — — — — — —		— — — Percent — — —	
Western Oregon:					
Douglas-fir	9,762,208	23,662	9,383	0.2	0.1
Engelmann spruce	1,544	<1			
Grand fir	64,404	<1			
Lodgepole pine	98,731	3,754	3,803	3.8	3.8
Mountain hemlock	302,147	<1			
Noble fir	85,062	<1			
Pacific silver fir	264,238	<1			
Ponderosa pine	92,401	<1			
Shasta red fir	54,049	<1			
Sitka spruce	168,951	<1			
Subalpine fir	24,044	<1			
Western hemlock	739,274	<1			
Western larch	<1	<1			
White fir	255,912	<1			
Other conifers	422,669	<1			
Hardwood, juniper, and nonstocked	2,764,207	13,982	11,839	0.5	0.4
All forest types	15,099,841	41,398	15,578	0.3	0.1

SE = standard error.

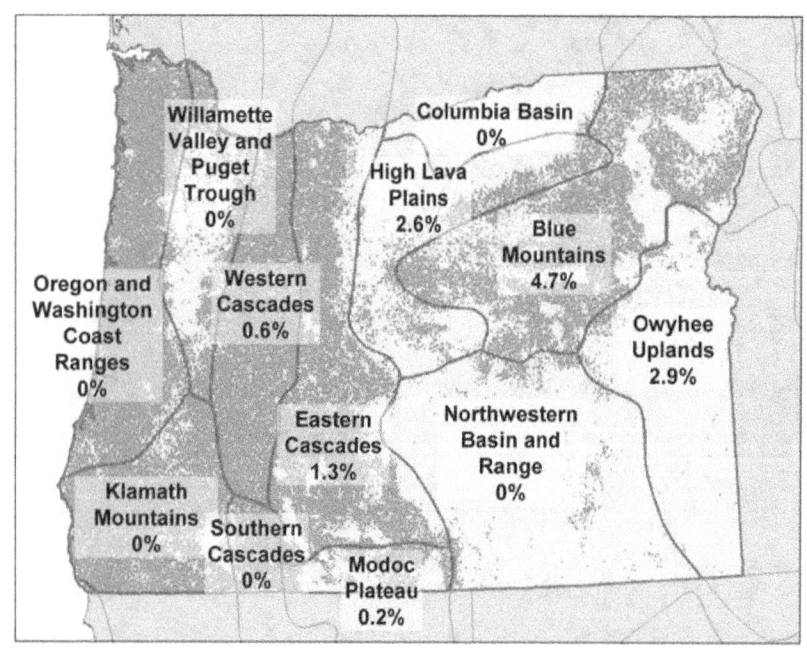

Figure 3—Percentage of conifer forest type within ecosection with >25 percent 10-year mortality from bark beetles.

numbers of other conifers present. In fact, of all the mortality attributed to bark beetles in larch stands, over 80 percent was in species other than larch. Over half of the beetle-caused mortality in larch stands was recorded on grand fir, white fir, and subalpine fir.

In general, mortality from bark beetles was lower on private lands than on public ownership (table 13). Forest Service lands are estimated to have 55 percent of the state's conifers but 83 percent of the beetle-caused mortality. About 90 percent of the board foot volume killed by bark beetles occurred on Forest Service lands (table 14). Bark beetles tend to prefer host trees that are less vigorous and therefore less able to repel their attacks. Generally, private landowners are motivated by economic reasons to harvest their stands before tree densities reduce tree vigor. Also, trees salvaged before the plots are remeasured would be recorded as harvested and not as mortality. Most of the public ownership in Oregon is Forest Service, which in recent years has been less aggressive in harvesting. Also, private forest land tends to be at lower elevations and of higher productivity than Forest Service lands (Donnegan et al., in press).

Defoliators—

Defoliating insects are generally a more serious problem in eastern than western Oregon (table 15). In eastern Oregon, the tree species with the most defoliation damage recorded are grand fir, subalpine fir, Douglas-fir, Pacific silver fir, and Engelmann spruce. For these species, all but Douglas-fir had much higher rates of defoliation at the time of first measurement. Western hemlock had a high estimate of defoliation in eastern Oregon, but this estimate is associated with a large standard error. White fir defoliation increased from the time of first measurement to the second (table 15).

Important defoliating insects in Oregon forests include the western spruce budworm *Choristoneura occidentalis* Freeman, Modoc budworm *C. retiniana* Walsingham, Douglas-fir tussock moth *Orgyia pseudotsugata* McDunnough, western hemlock looper *Lambdina fiscellaria lugubrosa* Hulst, and larch casebearer *Coleophora laricella* Hübner. Assessment of defoliator damage on forest inventory plots is made difficult by the time lapse between measurement of plots. Unless a crew happens to visit a plot within a few years of defoliation, the evidence of the defoliation will be hidden by new growth, and identification of a specific responsible insect would have to be conjecture based on history of the area and the host affected.

About 90 percent of the board foot volume killed by bark beetles occurred on Forest Service lands.

Table 13—Number of live conifers ≥5 inches diameter at breast height at first measurement (1984–1997) and annual conifer mortality from bark beetles, by ownership and region, 1984–2003

Ownership	Live trees	SE	Annual mortality from bark beetles	SE	Annual proportion killed by bark beetles	SE
	――――――― Thousand trees ―――――――				――― Percent ―――	
All Oregon:						
BLM	264,770	12,183	128	39	0.5	0.2
National forest	1,770,388	22,933	5,376	379	3.0	0.2
Other public	109,257	11,359	21	18	0.2	0.2
All public owners	2,144,415	28,344	5,524	381	2.6	0.2
Private, nonindustrial	378,717	19,540	283	85	0.8	0.2
Private, industrial	670,172	26,252	647	208	1.0	0.3
All private owners	1,048,888	32,373	930	225	0.9	0.2
All owners	3,193,304	42,756	6,454	442	2.0	0.1
Eastern Oregon:						
BLM	33,979	5,055	21	18	0.6	0.5
National forest	1,010,630	17,162	4,909	370	4.9	0.3
Other public	10,047	3,121	19	18	1.9	1.6
All public owners	1,054,656	18,161	4,950	371	4.7	0.3
Private, nonindustrial	180,363	11,668	268	84	1.5	0.5
Private, industrial	172,203	10,800	519	152	3.0	0.9
All private owners	352,565	15,160	786	174	2.2	0.5
All owners	1,407,221	23,260	5,736	410	4.1	0.3
Western Oregon:						
BLM	230,791	11,085	107	34	0.5	0.2
National forest	759,758	16,246	466	81	0.6	0.1
Other public	99,210	10,922	1	1	<0.1	<0.1
All public owners	1,089,760	22,497	574	88	0.5	0.1
Private, nonindustrial	198,354	15,674	15	10	0.1	0.1
Private, industrial	497,969	23,928	129	142	0.3	0.3
All private owners	696,323	28,604	144	142	0.2	0.2
All owners	1,786,082	36,327	718	167	0.4	0.1

SE = standard error

BLM = Bureau of Land Management

Table 14—Volume of live conifers ≥9 inches diameter at breast height at first measurement (1984–1997) and annual conifer mortality from bark beetles, by ownership and region, 1984–2003

Ownership	Live trees	SE	Annual mortality from bark beetles	SE	Annual proportion killed by bark beetles	SE
	———————— *Million board feet* —————————				——— *Percent* ———	
All Oregon:						
BLM	46,367	2,732	6	3	0.01	0.01
National forest	254,485	4,573	502	40	0.19	0.02
Other public	13,338	1,748	2	1	0.01	0.01
All public owners	314,190	5,607	510	40	0.16	0.01
Private, nonindustrial	27,827	1,702	14	5	0.04	0.01
Private, industrial	53,072	3,147	16	5	0.03	0.01
All private owners	80,899	3,572	30	7	0.03	0.01
All owners	395,089	6,638	540	41	0.13	0.01
Eastern Oregon:						
BLM	1,492	331	4	2	0.25	0.15
National forest	85,328	2,098	387	33	0.45	0.04
Other public	604	250	1	1	0.16	0.12
All public owners	87,425	2,139	392	33	0.45	0.04
Private, nonindustrial	10,644	811	13	4	0.12	0.04
Private, industrial	8,213	564	12	3	0.15	0.04
All private owners	18,858	966	25	6	0.13	0.03
All owners	106,282	2,326	417	34	0.39	0.03
Western Oregon:						
BLM	44,874	2,712	3	1	0.01	0
National forest	169,157	4,153	115	22	0.07	0.01
Other public	12,734	1,730	1	1	0.01	0.01
All public owners	226,765	5,253	119	22	0.05	0.01
Private, nonindustrial	17,182	1,496	1	1	0.01	0
Private, industrial	44,859	3,097	4	3	0.01	0.01
All private owners	62,041	3,439	5	3	0.01	0.01
All owners	288,807	6,277	124	22	0.04	0.01

SE = standard error.

BLM = Bureau of Land Management.

Table 15—Percentage of trees ≥5 inches diameter at breast height with defoliator damage recorded at time of first plot measurement (1984–1997) and time of second plot measurement (1995–2003), by species

Tree species	All Oregon				Western Oregon				Eastern Oregon			
	At first sample	SE	At second sample	SE	At first sample	SE	At second sample	SE	At first sample	SE	At second sample	SE
					Percent							
Douglas-fir	3.1	0.2	2.2	0.3	0.9	0.2	0.2	0.1	15.2	1.3	15.4	2.0
Engelmann spruce	15.2	2.5	2.5	1.1	29.3	15.1	3.1	1.4	14.3	2.5	2.5	1.2
Grand fir	31.1	2.1	8.9	1.3	3.5	1.4	0.9	0.5	37.5	2.4	11.4	1.7
Lodgepole pine	1.9	0.4	3.2	0.6	0.2	0.1	0.5	0.3	2.1	0.4	3.5	0.7
Mountain hemlock	11.1	2.5	6.0	2.3	19.9	4.5	10.7	4.1	0.4	0.2	0.2	0.1
Noble fir	4.3	2.7	0.7	0.5	5.3	3.5	0.8	0.6	1.0	0.7	0.2	0.2
Pacific silver fir	19.2	4.0	7.3	2.8	19.2	4.5	7.6	3.1	19.4	8.4	4.4	3.8
Ponderosa pine	3.5	0.4	1.2	0.3	<0.1	<0.1	<0.1	<0.1	3.7	0.5	1.2	0.4
Shasta red fir	1.3	1.2	<0.1	<0.1	<0.1	<0.1	<0.1	<0.1	2.1	1.9	0.1	0.1
Sitka spruce	0.4	0.4	0.8	0.8	0.4	0.4	0.8	0.8	<0.1	<0.1	<0.1	<0.1
Subalpine fir	17.3	2.9	5.1	1.7	34.1	9.7	23.1	8.7	13.6	2.8	2.0	0.9
Sugar pine	<0.1	<0.1	<0.1	<0.1	<0.1	<0.1	0.1	0.1	<0.1	<0.1	<0.1	<0.1
Western hemlock	1.1	0.4	0.2	0.1	0.9	0.4	0.2	0.1	16.5	14.7	<0.1	<0.1
Western larch	1.9	0.4	5.2	2.5	13.5	10.9	6.3	5.1	1.8	0.4	5.2	2.5
White fir	4.7	1.1	12.8	3.2	1.0	0.5	0.4	0.2	6.3	1.5	18.2	4.3
Other pines	0.2	0.1	0.7	0.4	0.1	0.1	0.2	0.1	0.4	0.2	1.3	0.9
Other conifers	0.1	<0.1	0.1	0.1	0.1	0.1	<0.1	<0.1	<0.1	<0.1	0.5	0.5
All conifers	5.4	0.3	3.1	0.3	2.7	0.4	1.0	0.2	8.9	0.5	5.9	0.6
All hardwoods	0	<0.1	0.2	0.1	<0.1	<0.1	0.2	0.1	<0.1	<0.1	<0.1	<0.1

SE = standard error.

Based on the number of trees and acres affected, the most important defoliator in Oregon is the western spruce budworm (fig. 4). The preferred host trees in Oregon for the western spruce budworm are Douglas-fir, grand fir, white fir, sub-alpine fir, Engelmann spruce, and western larch. Other conifers are sometimes fed on when budworm populations are dense but are seldom seriously damaged. At endemic population levels, budworm does not usually cause mortality. However, when outbreaks are intense and long in duration, trees can be killed or weakened to the point where they succumb to other insects or diseases. The high rates of defoliation in these species at the time of first plot measurement can be explained by a major spruce budworm outbreak that concluded a few years before the plots were sampled. This outbreak began in the early 1980s, peaking in 1987 with almost 6 million acres having defoliation mapped by aerial survey, and then peaking again in 1991 with 4 million acres (fig. 5). From 1982 to 1992, spruce budworm damage was mapped on at least 1 million acres annually (fig. 6). The majority of this defoliation occurred in the Blue Mountains of the northeast. It should not be assumed that all defoliated trees within these areas died, but it is likely that many did either die directly from defoliation or were stressed to the point of succumbing to other insects or diseases.

The Blue Mountains, Owyhee Uplands, and High Lava Plains ecosections where the longest duration of defoliation was mapped also had the highest proportion of host mortality attributed to defoliation (table 16). Within the combined area of these three ecosections, about 0.1 percent of the host trees were killed annually by defoliators (table 17). Outside of these areas, little mortality was attributed to defoliators. The ecosections with the greatest spruce budworm defoliation in the early 1990s also had the greatest rates of bark beetle mortality detected on plots.

Balsam woolly adelgid—
The balsam woolly adelgid (*Adelges piceae* Ratzeburg) is an exotic insect introduced from Europe. This insect was first detected in Oregon in 1930 (Keen 1952). This insect feeds by inserting its mouthparts through the bark of true firs (*Abies* spp.) and sucking fluids from living tissue. As the insects feed, they secrete toxins into their host that disrupt normal cell growth resulting in deformity of twigs (known as "gouting") and of wood growth in boles. As growing branch tips become deformed, new growth is inhibited and tree crowns deteriorate. The most susceptible hosts for the balsam woolly adelgid in Oregon are subalpine fir, Pacific silver fir, and grand fir. After the balsam woolly adelgid's introduction into Oregon, the

The majority of the 1 million acres of annual spruce budworm damage 1982 to 1992 was in the Blue Mountains of the northeast.

Figure 4—Spruce budworm larva feeding on foliage.

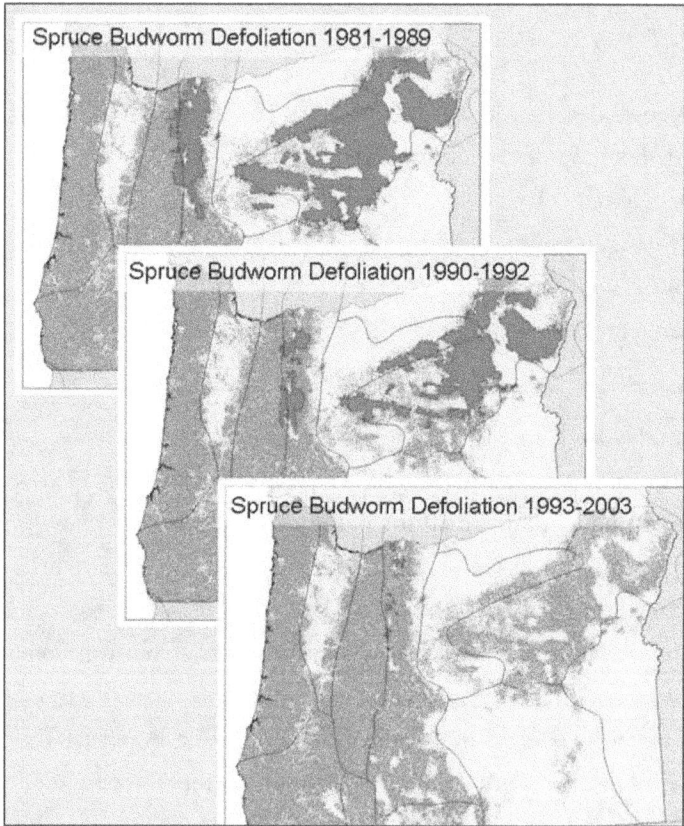

Figure 5—Distribution of spruce budworm defoliation mapped by aerial survey since 1981. Source: USDA FS 2007.

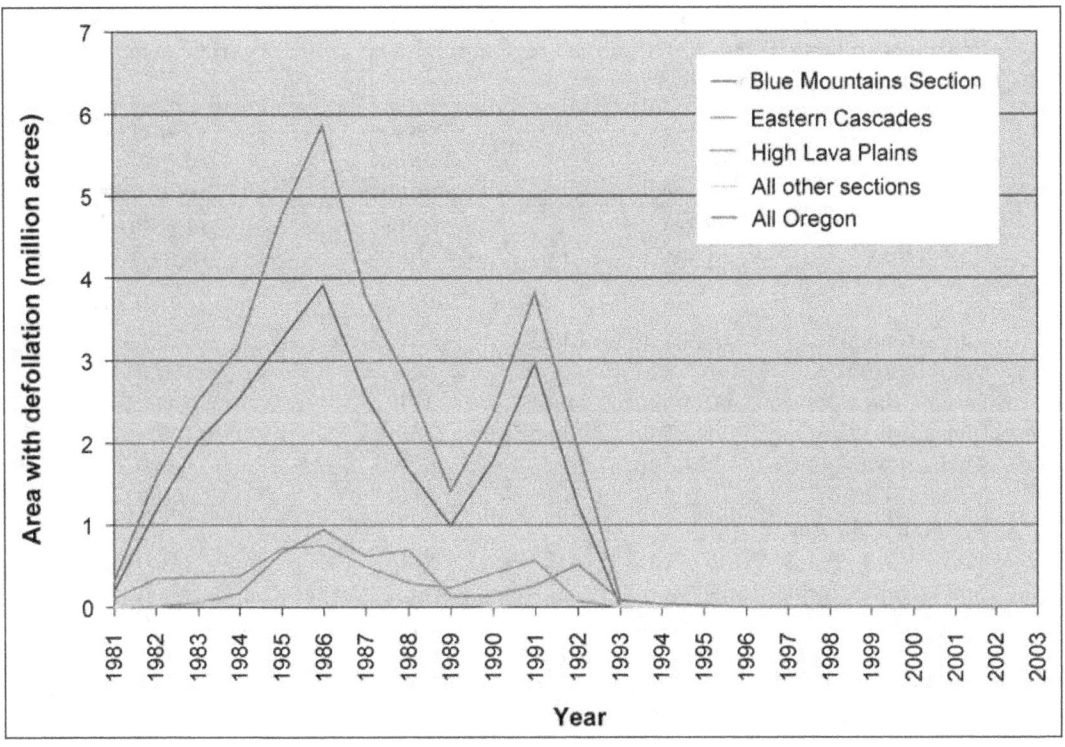

Figure 6—Area of spruce budworm defoliation detected by aerial survey, by ecosection and year. Source: USDA FS 2007.

Table 16—Average annual mortality and average annual mortality from defoliators, spruce budworm host species ≥5 inches diameter at breast height, by Bailey ecosection, 1984–2003

Ecosection	Average annual mortality	SE	Average annual mortality from defoliators	SE	Proportion of total mortality from defoliators	SE
	---------Thousand trees----------				----Percent-----	
Blue Mountains	5,246	400	271	84	5	2
Columbia Basin	<1		<1			
Eastern Cascades	2,263	267	11	9	1	0
High Lava Plains	699	179	226	100	32	12
Klamath Mountains	1,294	341	<1			
Modoc Plateau	184	50	<1			
Northern California Coast	<1		<1			
Northwestern Basin and Range	72	35	<1			
Oregon Coast Range	1,860	236	<1			
Owyhee Uplands	23	13	12	11	54	28
Southern Cascades	259	64	<1			
Western Cascades	2,632	243	16	9	1	0
Willamette Valley	601	183	<1			

SE = standard error.

Table 17—Number of live spruce budworm host ≥5 inches diameter at breast height at first measurement (1984–1997) and average annual host mortality from defoliators, by Bailey ecosection, 1984–2003

Ecosection	Live Host trees	SE	Average annual mortality from defoliators	SE	Proportion of live host trees killed annually by defoliators	SE
	– – – – – Thousand trees – – – – – –				– – – Percent – – –	
Blue Mountains	349,822	13,285	271	84	0.08	0.02
Columbia Basin	874	561	<1		<0.01	
Eastern Cascades	154,632	10,661	11	9	0.01	0.01
High Lava Plains	39,939	5,975	226	100	0.57	0.23
Klamath Mountains	284,586	15,639	<1		<0.01	
Modoc Plateau	25,323	4,255	<1		<0.01	
Northern California Coast	237	239	<1		<0.01	
Northwestern Basin and Range	9,796	5,675	<1		<0.01	
Oregon Coast Range	360,504	20,824	<1		<0.01	
Owyhee Uplands	3,267	1,053	12	11	0.38	0.30
Southern Cascades	59,145	8,468	<1		<0.01	
Western Cascades	306,761	13,965	16	9	0.01	<0.01
Willamette Valley	87,627	12,206	<1		<0.01	

SE = standard error.

Grand fir and silver fir declined after introduction of the balsam woolly adelgid.

abundance of grand fir and silver fir had declined greatly by the 1960s in the western Cascades, Willamette Valley, and Coast Range. This was because of both increased mortality and forest land managers being reticent to use these species for reforestation. In the past, subalpine fir functioned as a pioneer species in the Cascades, colonizing burns, avalanche tracks, and meadows. Subalpine fir abundance has declined in the Cascades, and fewer young trees are colonizing new areas. Since the 1970s, the adelgid has spread to eastern Oregon and can now be found in the Blue and Wallowa Mountains where significant mortality to subalpine fir has occurred (Overhulser 2004).

Damage caused by balsam woolly adelgid can be difficult for forest inventory crews to identify, and mortality may often be attributed to unknown causes. From 1998 to 2000, a statewide ground survey was conducted by Oregon Department of Forestry inventory crews specifically trained to determine the extent and severity of balsam woolly adelgid infestation (Overhulser 2004). They visited 859 plots with true fir. Balsam woolly adelgid was found on 325 of the plots (38 percent), and 50 of the plots had mortality attributed to balsam woolly adelgid (table 18).

Table 18—Plots with balsam woolly adelgid (BWA) detected and mortality from BWA, by Bailey ecosection

Ecosection	Plots sampled	Plots with BWA detected		Plots with BWA mortality	
	– – Number – –		*Percent*	*Number*	*Percent*
Blue Mountains	211	77	36	19	9
Eastern Cascades	108	70	65	17	16
High Lava Plains	6	4	67	0	0
Klamath Mountains	41	3	7	0	0
Modoc Plateau	1	0	0	0	0
Oregon Coast Ranges	144	25	17	0	0
Southern Cascades	8	0	0	0	0
Western Cascades	317	137	43	14	4
Willamette Valley	23	9	39	0	0
All Oregon	859	325	38	50	6

Source: Overhulser 2004.

The balsam woolly adelgid survey plots were established in areas where host trees were already known to be present. This strategy allows estimates to be made of the insects' distribution and severity of the insects' impact but does not allow direct estimates of area affected. Aerial survey has detected balsam woolly adelgid in Oregon for many years (fig. 7). Relatively few acres were mapped until recently. This increase is not due entirely to the spread of the insect into new areas. Aerial survey techniques for detecting balsam woolly adelgid damage have improved in recent years, making comparisons of acres mapped by year problematic. However the survey is still useful for tracking the distribution of the pest over time. The most infested acres mapped in any one year was 106,468 acres in 2003, with an average infestation area of 229 acres.

Diseases

Root Diseases—

At each forest inventory plot where crews detected root disease within the search radius of a subplot, the area within the search radius was classed as "root disease present" for the purposes of this assessment. The proportion of each plot represented by subplots with root disease was expanded to represent a portion of the total forest area of the state. Because the sampling density of plots differs, not all plots represent the same proportion of the total area. Within national forests, root disease was assessed by assigning a severity rating to the subplot when disease was detected. Outside national forests, root disease was sampled by mapping the extent of root

Figure 7—Distribution of balsam woolly adelgid detected by aerial survey 1980-2003. Mapped adelgid areas have been slightly enlarged on the map to make them visible at this scale. (Source: USDA FS 2007).

About 16 percent, or 4,790,669 acres, of the state's forest land was found to be associated with root disease.

disease pockets and recording the percentage of the subplot infected. As only one inventory directly recorded area and neither inventory recorded whether disease was present at subplot center, the estimates of root-disease-affected area developed here should be considered area **associated** with root disease and not area **of** root disease. Also, because inventory crews were often not allowed to cut into live trees to diagnose root disease, these estimates are likely to be conservative.

Overall, about 16 percent, or 4,790,669 acres, of the state's forest land was found to be associated with root disease (table 19). It should not be assumed that all trees on these acres are in immediate peril. Most of the damage done by root diseases occurs over decades to only a portion of the species that may be present in a stand. The Western, Eastern, and Southern Cascade ecosections were found to have the highest prevalence of root diseases. By forest type, true fir and mountain hemlock stands were found to have the most root disease present. These forest types had area associated with root disease significantly greater than 18 percent at

Table 19—Forested area associated with root disease, by Bailey ecosection, 1995–2003

| Ecosection | Forest area | | Forest area with root disease | | | |
	Total	SE	With root disease	SE	Proportion with root disease	SE
	— — — — — — — — — — —*Acres*— — — — — — — — — —				— —*Percent*— —	
Blue Mountains	5,838,099	102,780	635,070	40,366	10.9	0.7
Columbia Basin	26,521	14,442	1,808	1,654	6.8	5.2
Eastern Cascades	5,624,103	102,449	1,110,371	56,244	19.7	1.0
High Lava Plains	1,831,578	92,732	78,585	12,135	4.3	0.7
Klamath Mountains	4,031,655	105,195	280,654	30,620	7.0	0.7
Modoc Plateau	805,588	61,681	144,268	17,442	17.9	2.2
Northern California Coast	14,123	10,578	<1			
Northwestern Basin and Range	914,924	69,925	33,456	8,219	3.7	0.9
Oregon Coast Ranges	4,619,766	133,579	668,668	57,631	14.5	1.2
Owyhee Uplands	416,931	48,150	746	758	0.2	0.2
Southern Cascades	768,728	65,030	257,590	34,339	33.5	3.8
Western Cascades	4,270,462	105,469	1,446,692	60,772	33.9	1.4
Willamette Valley	1,028,981	87,038	132,761	29,931	12.9	2.7
All forest	30,191,457	146,793	4,790,669	116,263	15.9	0.4

SE = standard error.

the 66 percent confidence level (table 20). Of the mortality measured on forest inventory plots, approximately 9 percent was attributed to root disease (table 21). Annual volume loss to root disease is estimated at 213 million board feet per year (table 22). Unidentified root disease and armillaria were the root diseases most commonly recorded on plots.

In terms of number of trees and area impacted, the most important root diseases commonly found in Oregon are laminated root rot *Phellinus weirii* (Murr.) Gilb., annosus root disease *Heterobasidion annosum* (Fr.) Bref., armillaria root disease *Armillaria ostoyae* (Romagnesi) Herinck, and black stain root disease *Leptographium wageneri* (Kendrick) Wingfield (table 23). Although it is confined to a relatively small area, Port-Orford-cedar root disease *Phytophthora lateralis* Tucker & Milbrath is an introduced disease that is important in terms of its potential ecological impact. Laminated, annosus, and armillaria are wood-decaying fungi that consume the wood of the roots and lower boles that they colonize. These fungi can reduce the vigor of trees by interfering with the trees' ability to draw moisture through the roots to the crown (Goheen and Willhite 2006). Mortality can be

Table 20—Forested area associated with root disease, by forest type and region 1995–2003

Forest type	Forest area		With disease			
	Total	SE	Total	SE	Proportion	SE
	– – – – – – – – – – Acres – – – – – – – – – –				– – Percent – –	
All Oregon:						
Douglas-fir	11,494,127	180,201	2,159,299	89,279	19	1
Engelmann spruce	202,108	30,522	33,945	9,053	17	4
Grand fir	1,063,255	64,250	305,537	31,192	29	2
Lodgepole pine	1,638,876	83,077	189,746	23,916	12	1
Mountain hemlock	584,540	52,361	327,910	39,008	56	5
Noble fir	105,296	26,065	39,359	13,566	37	10
Pacific silver fir	289,938	39,104	129,337	25,233	45	6
Ponderosa pine	4,889,608	120,279	474,227	33,040	10	1
Shasta red fir	176,829	30,184	87,229	19,193	49	8
Sitka spruce	168,951	38,213	19,524	8,130	12	4
Subalpine fir	196,686	30,973	51,385	16,717	26	7
Western hemlock	762,160	69,682	143,933	26,302	19	3
Western larch	183,156	29,316	36,807	12,453	20	6
White fir	883,017	62,684	466,314	39,085	53	3
Other conifer forest types	516,124	56,390	67,020	18,032	13	3
Hardwood, juniper, and nonstocked	7,036,784	171,196	259,097	33,955	4	1
All Oregon	30,191,457	146,793	4,790,669	116,263	16	0
Eastern Oregon:						
Douglas-fir	1,731,919	84,226	238,744	25,822	14	1
Engelmann spruce	200,564	30,483	32,401	8,921	16	4
Grand fir	998,850	59,986	295,001	30,708	30	3
Lodgepole pine	1,540,146	80,055	162,864	21,452	11	1
Mountain hemlock	282,393	36,927	143,845	25,479	51	7
Noble fir	20,234	10,816	11,975	9,123	59	24
Pacific silver fir	25,700	13,039	23,448	12,565	91	9
Ponderosa pine	4,797,208	118,329	463,907	32,675	10	1
Shasta red fir	122,780	26,039	57,460	16,471	47	10
Subalpine fir	172,643	28,219	36,887	13,851	21	7
Western hemlock	22,886	10,920	10,759	6,245	47	23
Western larch	183,156	29,316	36,807	12,453	20	6
White fir	627,106	53,113	344,350	33,215	55	4
Other conifer forest types	93,456	22,733	20,400	9,498	22	9
Hardwood, juniper, and nonstocked	4,272,577	115,015	79,768	14,124	2	0
All eastern Oregon	15,091,616	114,401	1,958,615	67,649	13	0

Table 20—Forested area associated with root disease, by forest type and region 1995–2003 (continued)

Forest type	Forest area		With disease			
	Total	SE	Total	SE	Propor-tion	SE
	— — — — — — — — — — — *Acres* — — — — — — — — — —				— — *Percent* — —	
Western Oregon:						
Douglas-fir	9,762,208	159,874	1,920,555	85,526	20	1
Engelmann spruce	1,544	1,541	1,544	1,541	100	
Grand fir	64,404	23,042	10,536	5,517	16	8
Lodgepole pine	98,731	22,211	26,882	10,573	27	9
Mountain hemlock	302,147	37,478	184,065	29,537	61	6
Noble fir	85,062	23,739	27,383	10,041	32	10
Pacific silver fir	264,238	36,894	105,889	21,884	40	6
Ponderosa pine	92,401	21,589	10,320	4,899	11	5
Shasta red fir	54,049	15,337	29,770	9,882	55	10
Sitka spruce	168,951	38,213	19,524	8,130	12	4
Subalpine fir	24,044	12,766	14,498	9,359	60	25
Western hemlock	739,274	68,915	133,174	25,577	18	3
White fir	255,912	33,406	121,964	20,600	48	6
Other conifer forest types	422,669	51,615	46,620	15,327	11	3
Hardwood, juniper, and nonstocked	2,764,207	126,847	179,329	30,882	6	1
All western Oregon	15,099,841	99,501	2,832,053	95,285	19	1

SE = standard error.

Table 21—Average annual mortality of trees ≥5 inches diameter at breast height, by root disease and Bailey ecosection, 1984–2003

Ecosection	All causes Total	SE		Any root disease Total	SE	Proportion	SE
	Thousand trees			*Thousand trees*		*– – Percent – –*	
Blue Mountains	8,052	517		156	37	1.9	0.5
Columbia Basin	0						
Eastern Cascades	8,229	534		783	137	9.5	1.6
High Lava Plains	1,071	228		86	52	8.0	4.6
Klamath Mountains	3,163	427		231	81	7.3	2.5
Modoc Plateau	428	90		65	24	15.2	5.5
Northern California Coast	0						
Northwestern Basin and Range	231	82		23	14	10.1	6.3
Oregon Coast Ranges	5,205	528		584	159	11.2	2.8
Owyhee Uplands	146	73				0	
Southern Cascades	474	93		59	24	12.4	4.5
Western Cascades	6,247	451		842	138	13.5	2.0
Willamette Valley	966	237		118	58	12.2	5.5
All forest	34,212	1,125		2,946	278	8.6	0.8

Ecosection	Unknown root disease Total	SE	Proportion	SE	Annosus root disease Total	SE	Proportion	SE
	Thousand trees		*– – Percent – –*		*Thousand trees*		*– – Percent – –*	
Blue Mountains	51	21	0.6	0.3	19	12	0.2	0.1
Eastern Cascades	89	24	1.1	0.3	95	27	1.2	0.3
High Lava Plains	62	45	5.8	4.0				
Klamath Mountains	19	15	0.6	0.5				
Modoc Plateau	39	22	9.2	5.0	19	7	4.5	1.7
Northwestern Basin and Range	21	14	9.2	6.1				
Oregon Coast Ranges	89	70	1.7	1.3	50	35	1.0	0.7
Owyhee Uplands								
Southern Cascades	6	5	1.4	1.0	1	1	0.1	0.2
Western Cascades	290	80	4.6	1.2	22	14	0.4	0.2
Willamette Valley	9	12	0.9	1.2				
All forest	677	124	2.0	0.4	207	49	0.6	0.1

Table 21—Average annual mortality of trees ≥5 inches diameter at breast height, by root disease and Bailey ecosection, 1984–2003 (continued)

Ecosection	Armillaria root disease				Black stain root disease			
	Total	SE	Propor-tion	SE	Total	SE	Propor-tion	SE
	Thousand trees		*– – Percent – –*		*Thousand trees*		*– – Percent – –*	
Blue Mountains	86	26	1.1	0.3				
Eastern Cascades	484	114	5.9	1.3	4	3	0	0
High Lava Plains	1	1	0.1	0.1	23	25	2.1	2.3
Klamath Mountains	135	64	4.3	2.0				
Modoc Plateau	6	4	1.3	1.0				
Northwestern Basin and Range	2	2	0.9	0.9				
Oregon Coast Ranges	124	38	2.4	0.7				
Owyhee Uplands								
Southern Cascades	51	24	10.9	4.4				
Western Cascades	476	109	7.6	1.7				
Willamette Valley	5	6	0.5	0.6				
All forest	1,369	178	4.0	0.5	26	25	0.1	0.1

Ecosection	Laminated root rot				Port-Orford-cedar root disease			
	Total	SE	Propor-tion	SE	Total	SE	Propor-tion	SE
	Thousand trees		*– – Percent – –*		*Thousand trees*		*– – Percent – –*	
Blue Mountains								
Eastern Cascades	110	63	1.3	0.8				
High Lava Plains								
Klamath Mountains	70	46	2.2	1.5	6	6	0.2	0.2
Modoc Plateau	1	1	0.2	0.2				
Northwestern Basin and Range								
Oregon Coast Ranges	151	61	2.9	1.2	169	119	3.3	2.2
Owyhee Uplands								
Southern Cascades								
Western Cascades	54	19	0.9	0.3				
Willamette Valley	105	55	10.8	5.3				
All forest	491	115	1.4	0.3	176	119	0.5	0.3

SE = standard error.

Table 22—Average annual mortality volume of conifers ≥9 inches and hardwoods ≥11 inches diameter at breast height, by root disease and Bailey ecosection, 1984–2003

Ecosection	All causes			Any root disease			
	Total	SE		Total	SE	Propor-tion	SE
	Million board feet			Million board feet		– – Percent – –	
Blue Mountains	595	46		15	5	2.5	0.8
Columbia Basin	<1			<1			
Eastern Cascades	502	57		66	12	13.2	2.1
High Lava Plains	43	8		1	1	2.8	1.4
Klamath Mountains	124	19		8	4	6.6	2.9
Modoc Plateau	24	5		5	2	21.7	7.8
Northern California Coast	<1			<1			
Northwestern Basin and Range	12	4		1	0	5.7	3.5
Oregon Coast Range	260	34		24	6	9.1	2.3
Owyhee Uplands	4	1		<1			
Southern Cascades	55	11		10	3	17.4	4.9
Western Cascades	815	72		81	12	10.0	1.5
Willamette Valley	13	4		2	1	12.5	7.4
All forest	2,448	109		213	19	8.7	0.8

Ecosection	Unknown root disease				Annosus root disease			
	Total	SE	Propor-tion	SE	Total	SE	Propor-tion	SE
	Million board feet		– – Percent – –		Million board feet		– – Percent – –	
Blue Mountains	3	1	0.5	0.2	1	0	0.1	0.1
Eastern Cascades	5	1	1.0	0.3	12	5	2.5	0.9
High Lava Plains	1	1	2.0	1.3	<1			
Klamath Mountains	1	1	0.6	0.5	<1			
Modoc Plateau	2	1	8.9	3.8	2	1	8.0	4.4
Northwestern Basin and Range	1	0	4.9	3.1	<1			
Oregon Coast Range	3	2	1.2	0.7	3	2	1.1	0.8
Southern Cascades	1	1	2.0	1.5	<1	0	0.7	0.7
Western Cascades	33	7	4.1	0.8	3	2	0.4	0.3
Willamette Valley	1	1	4.2	5.2	<1			
All forest	50	7	2.1	0.3	21	6	0.9	0.2

Table 22—Average annual mortality volume of conifers ≥9 inches and hardwoods ≥11 inches diameter at breast height, by root disease and Bailey ecosection, 1984–2003 (continued)

Ecosection	Armillaria root disease				Black stain root disease			
	Total	SE	Proportion	SE	Total	SE	Proportion	SE
	Million board feet		*– – Percent – –*		*Million board feet*		*– – Percent – –*	
Blue Mountains	11	5	1.8	0.8	<1			
Eastern Cascades	44	10	8.8	1.8	<1	<1	<0.1	<0.1
High Lava Plains	<1	<1	0.2	0.2	<1	<1	0.5	0.6
Klamath Mountains	6	4	4.9	2.7	<1			
Modoc Plateau	1	1	3.6	2.5	<1			
Northwestern Basin and Range	<1	<1	0.8	0.8	<1			
Oregon Coast Range	10	3	3.7	1.3	<1			
Southern Cascades	8	3	14.7	4.6	<1			
Western Cascades	37	8	4.5	1.0	<1			
Willamette Valley	<1				<1			
All forest	117	15	4.8	0.6	<1	<1	<0.1	<0.1

Ecosection	Laminated root rot				Port-Orford-cedar root disease			
	Total	SE	Proportion	SE	Total	SE	Proportion	SE
	Million board feet		*– – Percent – –*		*Million board feet*		*– – Percent – –*	
Blue Mountains	<1				<1			
Eastern Cascades	5	2	0.9	0.5	<1			
High Lava Plains	<1				<1			
Klamath Mountains	<1	<1	0.3	0.3	1	1	0.8	0.8
Modoc Plateau	<1	<1	1.2	1.2	<1			
Northwestern Basin and Range	<1				<1			
Oregon Coast Range	7	4	2.6	1.5	1	1	0.5	0.4
Southern Cascades	<1				<1			
Western Cascades	8	4	1.0	0.5	<1			
Willamette Valley	1	1	8.3	5.6	<1			
All forest	22	6	0.9	0.3	2	1	0.1	0.1

SE = standard error.

Table 23—Total trees ≥5 inches diameter at breast height and number and proportion infected with root disease, by Bailey ecosection, 1995–2003

Ecosection	All causes			Any root disease			
	Total	SE		Total	SE	Propor-tion	SE
	Thousand trees			*Thousand trees*		*– – Percent – –*	
Blue Mountains	566,482	16,996		21,229	3,718	3.7	0.6
Columbia Basin	3,511	2,110		136	124	3.9	1.9
Eastern Cascades	697,304	20,595		63,181	6,196	9.1	0.8
High Lava Plains	66,097	6,389		1,348	404	2.0	0.6
Klamath Mountains	692,789	27,701		18,409	3,539	2.7	0.5
Modoc Plateau	70,862	7,054		11,015	2,377	15.5	3.1
Northern California Coast	2,965	2,570					
Northwestern Basin and Range	39,301	8,550		1,474	531	3.8	1.5
Oregon Coast Range	744,257	32,220		30,250	5,206	4.1	0.7
Owyhee Uplands	16,781	3,265					
Southern Cascades	100,216	10,719		9,961	2,411	9.9	2.3
Western Cascades	674,029	24,530		66,925	5,957	9.9	0.9
Willamette Valley	126,448	13,736		4,361	1,882	3.4	1.4
All forest	3,801,042	46,719		228,289	11,703	6	0.3

Ecosection	Unknown root disease				Annosus root disease			
	Total	SE	Propor-tion	SE	Total	SE	Propor-tion	SE
	Thousand trees		*– – Percent – –*		*Thousand trees*		*– – Percent – –*	
Blue Mountains	6,820	2,049	1.2	0.4	5,336	1,588	0.9	0.3
Eastern Cascades	10,722	2,034	1.5	0.3	12,401	2,254	1.8	0.3
High Lava Plains	472	197	0.7	0.3	188	142	0.3	0.2
Klamath Mountains	1,538	597	0.2	0.1	283	145	<0.1	0
Modoc Plateau	2,802	928	4.0	1.3	5,194	1,858	7.3	2.5
Northwestern Basin and Range	652	323	1.7	0.9	435	351	1.1	0.9
Oregon Coast Range	5,528	2,483	0.7	0.3	852	434	0.1	0.1
Southern Cascades	1,558	1,256	1.6	1.2	682	336	0.7	0.3
Western Cascades	24,444	3,337	3.6	0.5	3,463	1,178	0.5	0.2
Willamette Valley	38	49	<0.1	0				
All forest	54,573	5,327	1.4	0.1	28,833	3,572	0.8	0.1

Table 23—Total trees ≥5 inches diameter at breast height and number and proportion infected with root disease, by Bailey ecosection, 1995–2003 (continued)

	Armillaria root disease				Black stain root disease			
Ecosection	Total	SE	Propor-tion	SE	Total	SE	Propor-tion	SE
	Thousand trees		*– – Percent – –*		*Thousand trees*		*– – Percent – –*	
Blue Mountains	7,668	1,949	1.4	0.3				
Columbia Basin	136	124	3.9	1.9				
Eastern Cascades	30,355	4,121	4.4	0.6	145	107	<0.1	0
High Lava Plains	113	112	0.2	0.2	83	90	0.1	0.1
Klamath Mountains	11,854	2,748	1.7	0.4	2,292	1,926	0.3	0.3
Modoc Plateau	2,936	932	4.1	1.3				
Northwestern Basin and Range	382	186	1.0	0.5				
Oregon Coast Range	9,129	2,041	1.2	0.3	439	475	0.1	0.1
Southern Cascades	5,831	1,307	5.8	1.3	23	24	<0.1	0
Western Cascades	31,335	4,272	4.6	0.6	94	74	<0.1	0
Willamette Valley	2,132	1,042	1.7	0.8				
All forest	101,870	7,260	2.7	0.2	3,076	1,991	0.1	0.1

	Laminated root rot				Port-Orford-cedar root disease			
Ecosection	Total	SE	Propor-tion	SE	Total	SE	Propor-tion	SE
	Thousand trees		*– – Percent – –*		*Thousand trees*		*– – Percent – –*	
Blue Mountains	1,406	1,113	0.2	0.2				
Eastern Cascades	9,559	3,118	1.4	0.4				
High Lava Plains	492	200	0.7	0.3				
Klamath Mountains	1,330	529	0.2	0.1	1,112	418	0.2	0.1
Modoc Plateau	84	78	0.1	0.1				
Northwestern Basin and Range	5	5	<0.1	<0.1				
Oregon Coast Range	12,229	3,593	1.6	0.5	2,073	1,591	0.3	0.2
Southern Cascades	1,867	1,509	1.9	1.5				
Western Cascades	7,588	1,550	1.1	0.2				
Willamette Valley	2,191	1,152	1.7	0.9				
All forest	36,752	5,485	1.0	0.1	3,186	1,645	0.1	<0.1

SE = standard error.

caused either by destroying the roots' ability to translocate moisture or by weakening the tree structurally to the point that it uproots or breaks. Black stain root disease and Port-Orford-cedar root disease do not digest the structure of the wood they colonize but instead feed on sugars being translocated through the wood they invade. These fungi rapidly block a trees' internal plumbing and cause relatively quick mortality.

Annosus root disease in Oregon takes two forms: a "p-type" that infects pines and incense-cedar, and an "s-type" that infects spruce, true firs, Douglas-fir, red-cedar, and hemlocks. Species infected by the "s-type" annosus generally confine the rot to the metabolically inert inner sapwood and heartwood. Trees with this sort of infection are generally not killed directly by the fungus but become more susceptible to windthrow over time. In pines, annosus generally infects the water-translocating cambium and outer sapwood, resulting in more rapid decline and death. The spores of annosus are capable of infecting freshly cut stumps and growing inside for decades. For this reason, harvesting operations in infected stands tend to intensify the infection. This could partly explain the high incidence of root disease found in Shasta red fir and white fir stands where selective harvesting is common.

Armillaria root disease can infect most conifers to some degree. In its pathogenic forms, armillaria can cause relatively quick death in young trees, as the fungus kills the cambium of the root collar. In older trees, the infection is often restricted to the inner sapwood and heartwood allowing the trees to survive for many years with infection. There are several varieties of armillaria; some are rarely pathogenic or are pathogenic on some hosts and saprophytic on others. All can exist as saprophytes in dead wood for many years. When inventory crews attempt to determine the specific root disease causing mortality on a plot, they are generally prohibited from cutting into or excavating the roots of trees that are still alive. There are other common fungi in the *Armillaria* genus that could be confused with pathogenic armillaria but are generally saprophytes that would colonize only trees that were already dead or dying of other causes. The high rate of armillaria found on plots might be explained by crews being unable to distinguish saprophytic from pathogenic armillaria.

Black Stain root disease occurs in two varieties in Oregon. One variety typically infects Douglas-fir in western Oregon; the other infects mostly ponderosa and Jeffrey pines and occasionally other pines. This disease kills by plugging a tree's vascular tissues and does not rot infected wood. In recently killed trees, the disease can be identified by black staining of the sapwood, but this stain fades over time. Because this disease leaves no characteristic rot and inventory crews are prohibited from cutting into trees that are not yet dead, this disease is probably underrepresented in inventory data.

Laminated root rot is a common root rot of Douglas-fir, grand fir, white fir, and western hemlock. This rot kills trees by decaying the vascular tissues of the roots and by weakening the roots and lower boles of trees to the point that trees break or fall over. Laminated root rot can live for decades as a saprophyte in dead wood and can infect new trees as their roots grow into contact with the dead wood. In terms of mortality, growth loss, and area made inhospitable to regeneration, laminated root rot is the most serious damaging agent on Douglas-fir west of the Cascades (Kanaskie & Baer 1994).

Port-Orford-cedar root disease affects only a single host that is restricted to the southwest corner of the state. However it is a serious threat to that host and the ecosystems of which it is a component. This pathogen was introduced to Oregon within the last century, and very few Port-Orford-cedars have any resistance to this disease. When cedars are infected, the fungus rapidly plugs the tree's conductive tissues. This disease produces zoospores that can be spread great distances through the movement of water or soil.

On forest inventory plots, over 80 percent of the Port-Orford-cedar mortality was attributed to Port-Orford-cedar root disease (table 24). Overall, annual mortality of Port-Orford-cedar was about 1 percent. Most of this mortality was found in the Coast Range, with the annual rate of mortality about 3 percent. It should be noted that owing to the relatively few plots with this tree species, the sampling errors associated with these figures are relatively high (see "SE" column in table 24).

Root disease-bark beetle interaction—
Root disease can be a predisposing factor to successful bark beetle attack. Trees that have their vascular systems significantly damaged by root disease are generally less vigorous and will be less able to "pitch out" attacking beetles. Bark beetles often kill trees that were already in decline before attack. This interaction between bark beetles and root diseases often leads to disagreement as to whether the beetle or the fungus is ultimately responsible for tree death. It is possible that many trees killed by bark beetles had undetected root disease infections. In many cases, it is appropriate to consider bark beetles and root disease a single pest complex with mutual responsibility for tree death. Figure 8 displays the average annual mortality rate of trees in Oregon with bark beetle damage with and without root disease present.

Table 24—Number of live Port-Orford-cedar (POC) ≥5 inches diameter at breast height at time of measurement and average annual mortality from Port-Orford-cedar root disease, by Bailey ecosection (1984–2003)

Ecosection	Live 1984–1997		Live 1995–2003		Annual mortality		Annual mortality from POC root disease			
	Total	SE	Total	SE	Total	SE	Total	SE	Proportion	SE
	─────────────── Thousand trees ───────────────								Percent	
Oregon Coast Range	5,966	2,990	3,568	1,907	197	135	169	119	2.8	1.2
Klamath Mountains	7,944	1,646	10,068	2,587	8	7	1	1	<0.1	<0.1
All forest	13,909	3,396	13,637	3,191	205	136	171	119	1.2	0.7

SE = standard error.

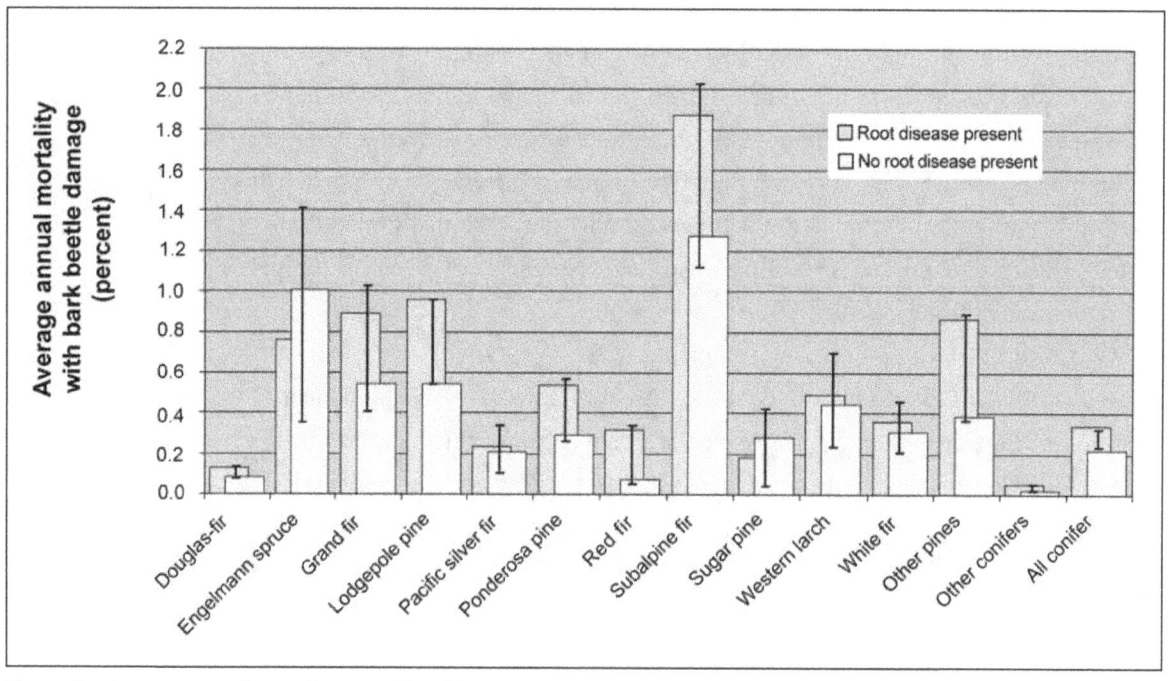

Figure 8—Average annual mortality rate of conifers with bark beetle damage, with and without root disease on the subplot, 1984–2003. Error bars indicate the standard error of the difference between paired columns.

Overall, conifers have higher estimated mortality associated with bark beetles when root disease is present on the subplot than when it is not.

Overall, conifers have higher estimated mortality associated with bark beetles when root disease is present on the subplot than when it is not (significant at the 66-percent level) (fig. 8). Lodgepole pine was the only individual species that was found to have statistically significant higher mortality from bark beetles in the presence of root disease. Estimates of bark beetle mortality by tree species where root disease is present are necessarily based on a relatively small number of plots, hence most individual species do not show a clear difference when the sizes of the standard errors are considered. However, except for sugar pine and Engelmann spruce, all major conifer species were estimated to have higher rates of bark beetle damage when root disease was present. In the case of sugar pine and Engelmann spruce, it is possible that not enough of these species were in the sample to make the expected pattern visible. Or, because sugar pine is seldom the majority species in a stand, when root disease was found near sugar pines, the disease was infecting other species in the stand and not the sugar pine. Having "s-type" annosus in a stand could actually benefit sugar pine by reducing competition from true firs and Douglas-fir. Grand fir, subalpine fir, and Engelmann spruce had relatively high rates of bark beetle prevalence whether or not root disease was on the subplot. In these species, susceptibility to bark beetle attack may be more influenced by the high stand densities and history of defoliation. Subalpine fir had the highest rate of bark beetle mortality overall.

Cankers and Galls—

At each inventory, individual trees were assessed for the presence of damaging cankers or galls. In conifers, the commonly encountered cankers and galls are caused by fungi. Many cankers and galls detected on plots could not be identified to species. Overall, about 3 percent of the state's conifers were found to be infected with a canker or gall of some kind (table 25).

The most common gall was the western gall rust *Endocronartium harknessii* (J.P. Moore) Y. Hiratsuka. This rust is common on ponderosa and lodgepole pines, causing globose swellings on infected limbs or stems (fig. 9). Seedlings and saplings can be killed by girdling stem infections. Larger trees are usually not killed by infections, but numerous infections can reduce vigor and predispose trees to bark beetle attack. Trunk infections can physically weaken the bole, making wind breakage more likely. Twenty percent of lodgepole pine was found to be infected with western gall rust. Even though lodgepole pine makes up only 9 percent of the state's conifers, over two-thirds of all the cankers and galls recorded on plots were recorded on this species. Commandra blister rust *Cronartium comandrae* Peck, stalictiform rust *C. coleosporiodes* Arthur, atropellis canker *Atropellis pinicola* Zeller & Goodding and *A. piniphilia* (Weir) Lohman & Cash were also found on lodgepole pine and together infect about 1 percent of the species. Ponderosa pine was found to be infected with the same rusts and cankers as lodgepole, but to a much lesser extent. Just 1 percent of the ponderosa was infected with any kind of canker or gall.

Even though lodgepole pine makes up only 9 percent of the state's conifers, over two-thirds of all the cankers and galls recorded on plots were recorded on this species.

Table 25—Trees ≥5 inches diameter at breast height and proportion of trees infected with cankers or galls, by species, 1995–2003

Tree species	Any canker or gall				Unknown canker or gall		Western gall rust		Commandra blister rust	
	Total	SE	Proportion	SE	Proportion	SE	Proportion	SE	Proportion	SE
	Thousand trees		- *Percent* -								
Douglas-fir	13,819	989	1.1	0.1	1.1	0.1				
Engelmann spruce	544	137	2.0	0.5	2.0	0.5				
Grand fir	1,148	361	0.7	0.2	0.7	0.2				
Lodgepole pine	72,054	4,316	24.9	1.2	3.4	0.4	20.3	1.1	0.1	<0.1
Mountain hemlock	1,493	368	1.2	0.3	1.2	0.3				
Noble fir	151	63	0.7	0.3	0.7	0.3				
Pacific silver fir	1,313	271	1.5	0.3	1.5	0.3				
Ponderosa pine	5,054	697	1.1	0.2	0.4	0.1	0.7	0.1	<0.1	<0.1
Shasta red fir	463	165	1.9	0.7	1.4	0.4				
Sitka spruce	60	40	0.3	0.2	0.3	0.2				
Subalpine fir	548	203	1.2	0.4	1.2	0.4				
Sugar pine	1,121	294	12.3	2.8	0.2	0.1				
Western hemlock	1,588	249	0.6	0.1	0.6	0.1				
Western larch	315	81	1.0	0.3	1.0	0.3				
Western white pine	2,680	450	25.0	3.9	0.5	0.3				
White fir	1,909	302	1.2	0.2	1.2	0.2				
Whitebark pine	365	124	4.7	1.6	1.4	0.6				
Other conifers	2,024	940	1.2	0.6	1.0	0.5	0.3	0.1		
All conifers	106,651	4,668	3.3	0.1	1.1	0.1	1.9	0.1	<0.1	0.1
All hardwoods	2,289	831	0.4	0.1	0.4	0.1			<0.1	<0.1

Table 25—Trees ≥5 inches diameter at breast height and proportion of trees infected with cankers or galls, by species, 1995–2003 (continued)

Tree species	Stalictiform rust		Atropellis canker		Cytospora or phomopsis		White pine blister rust		Gymnosporangium	
	Proportion	SE	Proportion	SE	Proportion	SE	Proportion	SE	Proportion	SE
Douglas-fir					<0.1	<0.1				
Engelmann spruce										
Grand fir					<0.1	<0.1				
Lodgepole pine	0.6	0.1	0.5	0.2						
Mountain hemlock										
Noble fir										
Pacific silver fir										
Ponderosa pine	<0.1	<0.1	<0.1	<0.1						
Shasta red fir					0.5	0.6				
Sitka spruce										
Subalpine fir										
Sugar pine							12.2	2.8		
Western hemlock										
Western larch							24.5	3.9		
Western white pine										
White fir					<0.1	<0.1				
Whitebark pine			0.5	0.5			2.8	1.4		
Other conifers									0.1	0.1
All conifers	0.1	<0.1	<0.1	<0.1	<0.1	<0.1	0.1	<0.1	<0.1	<0.1
All hardwoods										

SE = standard error.

Paul Dunham

Figure 9—Western gall rust infection on lodgepole pine.

White pine blister rust—

Although white pine blister rust *Cronartium ribicola* Fisch. infects less than 1 percent of the conifers in the state, it is the most important of the rusts recorded on
plots from an ecological standpoint. White pine blister rust is an introduced fungus
that causes cankers in our native five-needle pines: western white pine, sugar pine,
and whitebark pine. This rust was introduced on the west coast in 1910 and has
spread throughout the range of white pines in Oregon. Infections begin in the
needles and then spread into limbs. If an infection spreads to the bole of the tree
before the branch dies, the infection will eventually girdle the bole and kill the tree.
Small trees can be killed rapidly whereas larger trees may exist with branch infections for decades without succumbing. Host resistance to this rust is not common,

and this rust has the potential to greatly impact white pines as a significant component of their ecosystems (McDonald et al 2004).[1] On inventory plots, 24 percent of
the western white pine, 12 percent of the sugar pine, and 3 percent of the whitebark
pine were found to be infected with white pine blister rust (table 26). Although
western white pine is a valuable timber tree, it is now seldom planted in commercial
operations because of the risk of infection. Infection with white pine blister rust can
also predispose trees to attack by bark beetles.

There is not a large enough sample of infected whitebark and sugar pines to
determine conclusively whether infection rates and rates of mortality differ between regions of the state. Western white pine had an overall infection rate of 24
percent and a 37 percent infection rate in the Western Cascades ecosection. All
three white pine species had average annual mortality rates of about 2 percent.

Many trees with white pine blister rust coded at the first measurement that had
died before the second measurement had bark beetles coded for the cause of death.
Trees weakened by white pine blister rust are predisposed to bark beetle attack.
About 42 percent of all whitebark pine mortality was associated with bark beetle
damage, several times that attributed to cankers (table 27). The majority of this
can be attributed to the mountain pine beetle. Western white pine and sugar pine
mortality is about evenly divided between bark beetles and cankers. Bark beetles
and cankers accounted for about 70 percent of western white pine mortality and
about a quarter of sugar pine mortality.

Stem Decays—
There are many species of fungi that decay wood in Oregon's forests, the majority
of these fungi colonize and digest wood after the death of the tree. However, there
are many fungi that can colonize trees that are still alive. Stem decays that affect
living trees are usually confined to the heartwood and inner sapwood so that they do
not directly impact the vigor of trees. Generally, the most common stem decays do
not directly kill trees but instead weaken them mechanically so that they are at
greater risk to windthrow or breakage. Most stem decays require a tree to be
wounded in some way so that the fungi can colonize exposed heartwood or dead
sapwood (Goheen and Willhite 2006). Root diseases that cause stem decay are an

**Trees weakened by
white pine blister
rust are predis-
posed to bark beetle
attack.**

---

[1] Efforts to evaluate and develop resistance to white pine blister rust in western five-needle
pines are being conducted at the Dorena Genetic Resource Center, USDA Forest Service.
http://www.fs.fed.us/r6/dorena/rust/.

Table 26—White pine blister rust infection rates (1995–2003) and rates of mortality (all causes, 1984–2003) for trees ≥5 inches diameter at breast hieght, by Bailey ecosection

Species and ecosection	All live		Infected with blister rust				Average annual mortality			
	Total	SE	Total	SE	Proportion	SE	Total	SE	Proportion	SE
	– – – – – – Thousand trees – – – – – –				– – Percent – –		Thousand trees		– – Percent – –	
Whitebark pine:										
Blue Mountains	3,929	1,225	41	41	1.0	1.1	82	26	2.1	0.8
Eastern Cascades	3,819	880	158	94	4.1	2.5	48	18	1.3	0.4
Modoc Plateau	12	12								
Southern Cascades	12	9								
Western Cascades	66	57	19	19	29.1	5.2	20	17	30.0	32.5
All Oregon	7,839	1,509	218	105	2.8	1.4	149	36	1.9	0.5
Western white pine:										
Blue Mountains	28	26	8	8	28.4	2.5	5	5	17.4	23.3
Eastern Cascades	3,014	451	545	169	18.1	4.9	81	26	2.7	0.9
Klamath Mountains	4,061	1,382	968	332	23.8	8.3	58	25	1.4	0.7
Modoc Plateau	290	125					2	2	0.6	0.5
Southern Cascades	637	238	100	43	15.7	5.8	8	5	1.3	0.7
Western Cascades	2,692	425	1,001	243	37.2	6.3	78	18	2.9	0.6
All Oregon	10,722	1,532	2,622	446	24.5	3.9	231	41	2.2	0.4
Sugar pine:										
Eastern Cascades	3,474	751	500	239	14.4	5.9	12	7	0.3	0.2
Klamath Mountains	3,874	618	387	141	10.0	3.0	127	52	3.3	1.4
Modoc Plateau	335	202	12	12	3.7	4.1			<0.1	<0.1
Southern Cascades	519	293	4	4	0.7	0.8	3	3	0.6	0.6
Western Cascades	880	201	201	97	22.8	7.3	42	17	4.8	1.4
All Oregon	9,082	1,053	1,104	294	12.2	2.8	183	55	2.0	0.6

SE = standard error.

Table 27—Annual mortality and proportion of total mortality of whitebark, western white, and sugar pines ≥5 inches diameter at breast hieght from cankers and bark beetles, by Bailey ecosection

Species and ecosection	Annual mortality		Cankers				Bark beetles			
	Total	SE	Total	SE	Proportion	SE	Total	SE	Proportion	SE
	– – – – – – Thousand trees – – – – – –				*– – Percent – –*		*Thousand trees*		*– – Percent – –*	
Whitebark pine:										
Blue Mountains	82	26	3	3	3.6	3.5	50	20	61.8	12.5
Eastern Cascades	48	18	8	9	16.7	15.6	12	5	24.9	7.1
Western Cascades	20	17			<0.1	<0.1			<0.1	<0.1
All Oregon	149	36	11	9	7.3	5.9	62	20	41.8	9.8
Western white pine:										
Blue Mountains	5	5			<0.1	<0.1	1	1	15.2	21.4
Eastern Cascades	81	26	11	6	14.2	7.5	42	18	52.0	10.0
Klamath Mountains	58	25	35	21	61.4	20.2	11	8	18.8	10.1
Modoc Plateau	2	2			<0.1	<0.1			<0.1	<0.1
Southern Cascades	8	5	1	1	10.9	12.3	7	5	85.2	11.8
Western Cascades	78	18	43	15	55.1	10.6	9	3	11.4	4.3
All Oregon	231	41	91	27	39.2	8.7	70	20	30.1	6.3
Sugar pine:										
Eastern Cascades	12	7			0	0	10	6	82.9	16.1
Klamath Mountains	127	52	6	6	5.0	5.0	11	9	8.5	7.1
Southern Cascades	3	3			0	0	2	2	67.8	34.4
Western Cascades	42	17	15	11	35.1	19.9	6	3	15.1	7.8
All Oregon	183	55	21	12	11.5	6.8	29	11	15.7	6.9

SE = standard error.

exception in that they can colonize the bole of the tree through infected roots. Schweinitzii butt rot *Phaeolus schweinitzii* (Fr.) Pat., laminated root rot, and annosus root disease commonly cause butt decay in infected trees.

Stem decays reduce both the quality and quantity of wood that can be harvested from trees. Stem decay fungi are commonly divided into "brown rots" and "white rots" depending on the components of the wood they consume. Brown rots digest the cellulose that makes up the bulk of the cell walls of wood but leave the brown lignin undigested. White rots consume the lignin as well as the cellulose. As decay fungi colonize wood, initially there may be only a discoloration of the wood with little loss of strength. But as a fungus digests more material, the wood will progressively weaken. Eventually brown rots will cause the wood to crack into crumbling blocks. White rots will degrade wood into a stringy or spongy mass, and voids may enlarge and coalesce (Goheen and Willhite 2006). Although stem decays can hasten tree death and degrade their utility for commercial use, they are valuable for nutrient cycling and for creating wildlife habitat. Several species of birds and mammals depend on trees hollowed by decay. Several bird species excavate their nesting cavities in trees with interiors softened by stem decays (Bull et al. 1997).

Field inventory crews assessed each tree for indications of stem decay such as conks, old broken tops, or old wounds; 3 percent of the trees sampled had some outward sign of decay. The proportion of trees with detectable decay differed by ownership. Trees on national forest and BLM lands had indicators of rot more often than trees on private lands, (about 4 percent and 2 percent, respectively) (table 28). The frequency and severity of stem decays often increases with stand maturity (Filip and Schmitt 1990). Older trees have been exposed to more injuries, and decays have had longer to progress. Donnegan (in press) found that the vast majority of forest with stand ages greater than 160 years is found on public lands.

Crews recorded the specific decay organism on trees if conks or characteristic decay allowed identification. In most cases specific rots were not identified. The most commonly recorded stem decay in Oregon was red ring rot *Phellinus pini* (Thore:Fr.). This fungus accounted for 13 percent of all rots seen on conifers and about 41 percent of the decay recorded for Douglas-fir (table 29). Rusty red stringy rot *Echinodontium tinctorium* (Ellis & Everh.) Ellis & Everh. was commonly detected in true firs and hemlocks. Eighteen percent of the rots detected in mountain hemlock and 11 percent of the rots detected in grand fir was attributed to this fungus. Schweinitzii butt rot was common only on Douglas-fir, accounting for 4 percent of the rots detected on this species.

The incidence of stem decay is certainly higher than what inventory crews can detect by examining the exterior of trees. Wounds high in trees can be difficult to observe, and diagnostic conks will not always be present. Aho (1966, 1974) and Aho and Simonski (1975) conducted several studies of important Oregon conifers to build regression equations to estimate defect in trees based on species, age, diameter, and outward indicators of decay (if visible). These equations are used by FIA to calculate hidden decay in trees, and I have applied them to trees sampled on BLM and Forest Service plots as well. This technique allows decay to be estimated for trees even where no decay was visible to the crews. Where decay was visible to crews, I used their estimate if it was larger than the equation prediction for hidden decay. Using these methods, the estimate of board foot volume lost to stem decay is 7 percent of the gross volume (table 30). National forest ownership had the largest volume deduction, and private industry had the lowest (about 8 percent and 4 percent, respectively). Grand fir and mountain hemlock were both estimated to have volume loss owing to stem decays greater than 15 percent (table 31). Engelmann

Seven percent of the gross board foot volume is lost to stem decay: 8 percent of national forests and 4 percent of private industrial land.

Table 28—Live trees ≥5 inches diameter at breast hieght at second measurement and trees with observed stem decay, by owner and decay type

Ownership	All trees		Red ring rot		Rust red stringy rot		Schweinitzii butt rot		Unidentified rot		Any observed stem decay			
	Total	SE	Total	SE	Total	SE	Total	SE	Total	SE	Total	SE	Proportion	SE
	---------- Thousand trees ----------												Percent	
Bureau of Land Management	418,120	14,693	2,546	374	12	11	213	95	15,417	1,366	18,112	1,479	4.3	0.4
National forest	1,905,621	23,968	4,859	341	2,456	310	439	70	62,842	2,330	70,445	2,405	3.7	0.1
Other public	161,764	12,604	632	394			8	8	3,406	1,028	4,046	1,131	2.5	0.7
All public owners	2,485,505	30,809	8,038	641	2,469	310	660	118	81,665	2,890	92,602	3,041	3.7	0.1
Private, nonindustrial	470,811	21,158	847	535	47	25	11	11	11,595	3,374	12,501	3,474	2.7	0.7
Private, industrial	844,727	28,810	761	209	103	64	204	142	12,606	1,859	13,490	1,919	1.6	0.2
All private owners	1,315,538	35,580	1,607	574	150	69	215	142	24,201	3,853	25,990	3,969	2.0	0.3
All owners	3,801,042	46,719	9,645	861	2,618	318	875	185	105,866	4,816	118,593	5,000	3.1	0.1

SE = standard error.

Table 29—Live trees ≥5 inches diameter at breast hieght at second measurement and trees with observed stem decay, by species and decay type

Species	All trees		Red ring rot		Rust red stringy rot		Schweinitzii butt rot		Unidentified rot		Any observed stem decay			
	Total	SE	Total	SE	Total	SE	Total	SE	Total	SE	Total	SE	Proportion	SE
	――――――――――――――――――――――――― Thousand trees ―――――――――――――――――――――――――												Percent	
Douglas-fir	1,292,955	28,902	8,978	854			827	182	12,580	801	22,041	1,278	1.7	0.1
Engelmann spruce	27,221	2,845							205	56	205	56	0.8	0.2
Grand fir	169,121	9,065	35	11	577	114	27	20	4,818	468	5,439	503	3.2	0.3
Lodgepole pine	289,787	13,004	53	28					8,694	1,083	8,742	1,083	3.0	0.4
Mountain hemlock	127,062	9,938	61	25	726	219			3,366	403	4,140	515	3.3	0.3
Noble fir	23,187	4,225	4	4	20	9			427	103	451	104	1.9	0.5
Pacific silver fir	90,334	8,049			82	44			1,977	316	2,059	326	2.3	0.3
Ponderosa pine	456,385	12,868	75	29			4	4	3,281	211	3,360	213	0.7	0
Shasta red fir	24,043	3,507	4	4	121	55			916	184	1,041	199	4.3	0.7
Sitka spruce	21,336	4,577	34	27					47	27	81	53	0.4	0.2
Subalpine fir	46,384	5,050			41	23			853	171	894	173	1.9	0.4
Sugar pine	9,082	1,053	44	22			2	2	279	71	323	75	3.6	0.8
Western hemlock	275,408	16,943	182	47	497	119	12	9	6,619	701	7,300	723	2.7	0.3
Western larch	31,752	3,188							315	60	315	60	1.0	0.2
White fir	158,830	9,439	124	40	554	101	4	4	6,459	495	7,123	536	4.5	0.3
Other pines	25,119	2,914	44	45					1,665	342	1,710	347	6.8	1.2
Other conifers	159,944	8,576	8	6					10,084	793	10,088	793	6.3	0.5
All conifers	3,227,948	41,975	9,645	861	2,618	318	875	185	62,585	1,999	75,311	2,276	2.3	0.1
All hardwoods	573,094	22,932							43,281	4,326	43,281	4,326	7.6	0.7
All trees	3,801,042	46,719	9,645	861	2,618	318	875	185	105,866	4,816	118,593	5,000	3.1	0.1

SE = standard error.

Table 30—Volume of conifers ≥9 inches and hardwoods ≥11 inches diameter at breast height at second measurement, volume after deduction for stem decay, and proportion with decay, by owner

Ownership	Gross volume		Volume after rot deducted		Proportion of gross volume with decay	
	Total	SE	Total	SE	Prop.	SE
	- - - - - - - *Million board feet* - - - - - - - -				*Percent*	
Bureau of Land Management	54,799	2,761	51,687	2,536	5.7	0.4
National forest	268,519	4,612	246,433	4,151	8.2	0.2
Other public	19,282	1,786	18,294	1,665	5.1	1.0
All public owners	342,600	5,664	316,414	5,141	7.6	0.2
Private, nonindustrial	32,721	1,930	31,066	1,850	5.1	0.5
Private, industrial	53,151	2,656	51,107	2,580	3.8	0.4
All private owners	85,872	3,280	82,172	3,172	4.3	0.3
All owners	428,473	6,533	398,586	6,029	7.0	0.1

SE = standard error.   Prop. = proportion

Table 31—Volume of conifers ≥9 inches and hardwoods ≥11 inches diameter at breast height at second measurement, volume after deduction for stem decay, and proportion with decay, by species

Tree species	Gross volume		Volume after rot deducted		Proportion of gross volume with decay	
	Total	SE	Total	SE	Prop.	SE
	- - - - - - - *Million board feet* - - - - - - - -				*Percent*	
Douglas-fir	233,212	5,308	220,338	4,995	5.5	0.1
Engelmann spruce	4,019	455	3,388	384	15.7	0.9
Grand fir	17,816	1,081	14,974	938	16.0	0.8
Lodgepole pine	7,001	385	6,840	375	2.3	0.4
Mountain hemlock	12,578	1,244	10,198	966	18.9	2.1
Noble fir	5,174	777	4,662	696	9.9	0.9
Pacific silver fir	6,606	693	6,001	629	9.2	0.7
Ponderosa pine	39,578	1,015	39,037	1,000	1.4	0.1
Shasta red fir	5,320	847	4,551	726	14.5	1.1
Sitka spruce	4,707	984	4,529	935	3.8	0.7
Subalpine fir	1,572	199	1,347	170	14.3	1.0
Sugar pine	3,480	330	3,315	313	4.7	0.6
Western hemlock	31,202	1,671	29,398	1,586	5.8	0.5
Western larch	4,356	362	4,187	349	3.9	0.5
White fir	14,855	976	12,670	821	14.7	0.8
Other pines	2,094	181	1,987	173	5.1	0.6
Other conifers	12,933	810	11,394	692	11.9	0.9
All conifers	406,503	6,382	378,816	5,894	6.8	0.2
All hardwoods	21,969	1,155	19,771	1,024	10.0	0.7
All trees	428,473	6,533	398,586	6,029	7.0	0.1

SE = standard error.   Prop. = proportion

spruce, Shasta red fir, subalpine fir, and white fir had volume losses greater than 10 percent. Pines, Sitka spruce, Douglas-fir, and western larch had lower than the average loss to decay for conifers as a group (table 31). These differences are significant at the 66-percent confidence level. Of the total volume deducted for decay, 45 percent was detected by crews (table 32).

Foliar Pathogens—

There are several common diseases of Oregon forests that infect the foliage and twigs of forest trees. Field crews searched for damage from rhabdocline needle cast *Rhabdocline pseudotsugae* Syd., elytroderma needle blight *Elytroderma deformans* (Weir) Darker, Swiss needle cast *Phaeocryptopus gaeumannii* (Rohde) Petrak, and other broom rusts. These fungi can cause deterioration of crowns and growth loss but seldom cause significant levels of mortality. Overall, less than 1 percent of trees sampled had any foliar pathogen recorded (table 33). Nearly all foliar pathogens recorded were classified as "unknown." It is likely that infection rates of foliar pathogens are greater than what is recorded on forest inventory plots. The symptoms of these diseases are often subtle or can be confused with other conditions.

From 1996 through 2006 an average of 236,000 acres of Swiss needle cast damage was mapped each year.

Of the foliar pathogens, Swiss needle cast is the most important in terms of area affected and total growth loss (Maguire et al. 2002). Swiss needle cast is a native fungus common in the Oregon coast range where it infects Douglas-fir. This disease has become more prevalent since the 1980s as the proportion of the forest that is predominately Douglas-fir has been increased by forest management practices. This disease is easily missed when looking up into trees from below or if observing at the wrong time of year. Swiss needle cast was not consistently searched for on forest inventory plots and is not included in table 33. Swiss needle cast is more easily detected and quantified by aerial surveys of specifically trained crews. Aerial survey probably underestimates the extent of Swiss needle cast because infections must cause extensive discoloration before it can be noticed from the air. Since 1996, the Oregon Department of Forestry has been conducting an aerial survey of western Oregon for Swiss needle cast. The 2006 survey detected 325,500 acres of Douglas-fir forest with obvious symptoms of Swiss needle cast. From 1996 through 2006, an average of 236,000 acres were mapped per year. The greatest number of acres mapped in any one year was 387,000 acres in 2002 (fig. 10), (Forest Insect and Disease Aerial Detection Survey).

Table 32—Volume of of conifers ≥9 inches and hardwoods ≥11 inches diameter at breast height at second measurement and volume deducted for stem decay, by owner, and decay type

Ownership	Gross volume		Total volume deducted for decay[a]		Red ring rot		Rust red stringy rot		Schweinitzii butt rot		Unidentified decay	
	Total	SE	Total	SE	Total	SE	Total	SE	Total	SE	Total	SE
					Million board feet							
Bureau of Land Management	54,799	2,761	3,111	308	955	196	5	8	19	7	708	87
National forest	268,519	4,612	22,086	685	1,594	135	1,290	182	151	30	6,707	313
Other public	19,282	1,786	989	232	160	107			7	8	195	53
All public owners	342,600	5,664	26,186	786	2,709	261	1,296	182	178	32	7,610	329
Private, nonindustrial	32,721	1,930	1,655	171	75	35	21	13	15	15	480	77
Private, industrial	53,151	2,656	2,045	211	192	55	54	30	39	29	699	126
All private owners	85,872	3,280	3,700	272	267	65	75	33	54	33	1,179	147
All owners	428,473	6,533	29,887	831	2,976	269	1,371	185	232	46	8,789	361

[a] Total volume deducted for decay includes hidden decay

SE = standard error.

Table 33—Live trees ≥5 inches diameter at breast height with foliar pathogens, and rate of infection, by species

Tree species	All live		Any foliar pathogen				Unknown foliar pathogen		Rhabdocline		Elytroderma		Broom rusts	
	Total	SE	Total	SE	Proportion	SE	Total	SE	Total	SE	Total	SE	Total	SE
	Thousand trees		*Thousand trees*		*Percent*		*Thousand trees*							
Douglas-fir	1,292,909	28,901	7,202	1,419	0.6	0.1	5,203	1,254	1,999	664				
Engelmann spruce	27,221	2,845	20	11	0.1	<0.1	20	11						
Grand fir	169,121	9,065	2,660	1,017	1.6	0.6	2,641	1,017					19	16
Lodgepole pine	289,787	13,004	610	329	0.2	0.1	534	320			76	77		
Mountain hemlock	127,062	9,938	35	28	<0.1	<0.1	35	28						
Noble fir	23,187	4,225	4	4	<0.1	<0.1	4	4						
Pacific silver fir	90,334	8,049	927	658	1.0	0.7	927	658						
Ponderosa pine	456,385	12,868	5,622	999	1.2	0.2	4,742	921			879	397		
Shasta red fir	24,043	3,507	4	4	<0.1	<0.1	4	4						
Sitka spruce	21,336	4,577												
Subalpine fir	46,384	5,050	336	153	0.7	0.3	196	84					140	128
Sugar pine	9,082	1,053	8	8	0.1	0.1	8	8						
Western hemlock	275,408	16,943	247	163	0.1	0.1	247	163						
Western larch	31,752	3,188	340	317	1.1	1.0	340	317						
Western white pine	10,722	1,532	9	9	0.1	0.1	9	9						
White fir	158,830	9,439	520	265	0.3	0.2	178	71					342	256
Whitebark pine	7,839	1,509	82	79	1.0	0.9	82	79						
Other conifers	166,502	8,795	334	117	0.2	0.1	334	117						
All conifers	3,227,902	41,975	18,959	2,221	0.6	0.1	15,504	2,043	1,999	664	955	404	501	299
All hardwoods	573,094	22,932	198	200	<0.1	<0.1	198	200						

SE = standard error.

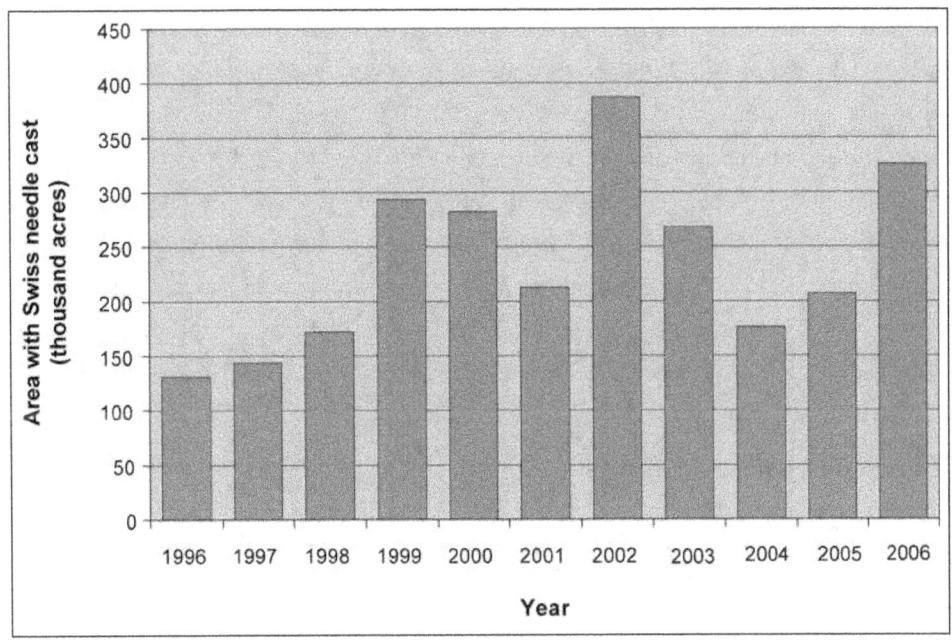

Figure 10—Area with Swiss needle cast mapped by aerial survey 1996-2006. Source: USDA FS 2007.

Sudden Oak Death—

Sudden oak death *Phytophthora ramorum* is an exotic pathogen of unknown origin. It was first noticed killing trees in the mid 1990s in coastal counties of California. This disease causes lethal cankers in several species of trees native to Oregon: Tanoak, California black oak, and canyon live oak. This disease can also cause foliar symptoms in California-laurel and Douglas-fir, and shoot dieback and foliage infections in a wide variety of understory vegetation such as rhododendron (*Rhododendron macrophyllum* D. Don ex G. Don) and evergreen huckleberry (*Vaccinium ovatum* Pursh). This pathogen has already caused widespread mortality of oaks and tanoaks in coastal California from southern Monterey County to southern Humboldt County (Mai et al. 2006). The disease has been found to infect commercial nursery stock causing economic losses to that industry through the loss of inventory, quarantines, and inspections. The disease has tremendous potential to be destructive in Oregon forests and nurseries. The tanoak is extremely susceptible to the disease, and with 345,000 acres of tanoak forest type in southwestern Oregon, it is one of the predominant hardwoods there (Campbell et. al. 2004).

Sudden oak death produces spores during wet weather that can be dispersed in running water or wind-driven rain or mist. The disease also produces a resting spore that can survive for months or years in soil or plant parts.

Sudden oak death was first discovered in Oregon in 2001 at five sites near the coastal town of Brookings at the southwestern corner of the state. Since the discovery of this disease in Oregon, federal and state agencies have cooperated in an effort to eradicate the disease in the state (Kanaskie et al. 2006). An 11-square-mile quarantine area was established surrounding the infected sites, and the infected sites were clearcut and burned to remove host species. New infection sites have been discovered every year since 2001, and the quarantine area had expanded to 22 square miles by 2006. The number of new infections and spread from old infection sites seem to be partly dependent on the weather; unusually wet weather in spring and early summer seems to favor spread of the disease. Eradication efforts have become more aggressive, including use of herbicides on nonfederal lands. Considering how quickly sudden oak death spread and intensified in California, the fact that the disease is still restricted to such a small area in Oregon is cause for hope.

Dwarf Mistletoe

Dwarf mistletoes (*Arceuthobium* spp.) found in Oregon are small, inconspicuous plants that are parasites of conifers (fig. 11). Dwarf mistletoe plants are obligate parasites and usually an individual species can infect only one or a few host species. When a dwarf mistletoe seed germinates at the base of a conifer needle, its growth penetrates the thin bark and establishes its root system within the host tree. The parasite may exist and grow for several years within the host before producing aerial shoots (Geils et al. 2002). Mature female plants produce seeds that are ejected by hydrostatic pressure. The seeds are sticky and will attach themselves to conifer needles they strike. Rainfall then washes some seeds down the needles into contact with a twig where they can successfully germinate. When ejected, the seeds can travel short distances to adjacent trees or establish new infections within the same tree.

Although the dwarf mistletoe plants themselves are inconspicuous, their effects on host trees can be dramatic. Mistletoe plants induce distorted growth at infection sites eventually causing dense tangles of limbs and foliage called witches' brooms or deformed and swollen stems (fig. 12). Although detrimental to the host tree, these witches' brooms can provide benefits to wildlife such as shelter to several species of small mammals and birds. Trees that are heavily parasitized will experience reduced growth and vigor as the trees' resources are diverted to growth of brooms (Hawksworth 1977).

On forest inventory plots, dwarf mistletoe infections on individual trees were rated using Hawksworth's Dwarf Mistletoe Rating system (DMR) (Hawksworth

Figure 11—Dwarf mistletoe infection in lodgepole pine.

Figure 12—Dwarf mistletoe infections in western larch. The larch on the left is only lightly infected in the upper crown with a broom in the lower crown. The other larches are heavily infected with brooms throughout their crowns.

1977). This system divides the tree's crown into thirds (top, middle, and bottom) with each third scored 0 for no mistletoe, 1 for less than half the branches infected, or 2 for more than half the branches infected or significant brooming present. The scores are then summed for the tree, a total score of 0 to 6 for the tree.

Statewide, 9 percent of the conifers tallied on plots had dwarf mistletoe infections (table 34). The tree species with the highest rates of infection were lodgepole pine, mountain hemlock, Pacific silver fir, ponderosa pine, western hemlock, and western larch. All these species had infection rates greater than 10 percent. About one-third of lodgepole pines and western larches were infected. Between the two times of plot measurement there was little change in the infection rates of most species. Mistletoe infections are much more common in east-side forest than in the west. Fifteen percent of conifers in eastern Oregon had mistletoe infection (table 35). Only 4 percent of those in western Oregon were infected (table 36). Ponderosa pine and Douglas-fir had drastically lower rates of infection in western Oregon compared to eastern Oregon. In western Oregon just 1 percent of these species were infected, whereas in east-side forests, 18 percent of Douglas-fir was infected and 13 percent of the ponderosa pine. Douglas-fir dwarf mistletoe (*Arceuthobium douglasii* Engelm.) is generally not found north of the Klamath and Siskiyou Mountains in western Oregon. Ponderosa pine is typically infected by the western dwarf mistletoe (*A. campylopodum* Engelm.). Where ponderosa pine occurs in west-side forests, it is often in mixed stands with Douglas-fir and white fir, which are not suitable hosts for the western dwarf mistletoe and can serve as barriers to its spread through a stand.

Mistletoe seldom kills trees directly but, by reducing tree vigor, makes them more vulnerable to insects, diseases, and drought. Although 9 percent of the state's live conifers were found to be infected, about 12 percent of conifers that died since the first measurement had dwarf mistletoe (significantly different at the 66 percent confidence level) (table 37). Over the sampling period, the mortality volume of conifers averaged 2.3 billion board feet per year. An average of 276 million board feet of annual mortality was infected with mistletoe (table 38). Comparing plots measured at two points in time allows a comparison of mortality rates between infected and uninfected trees over time. For the purpose of this comparison, I considered trees with DMR ratings of 1 or 2 to be lightly infected, ratings of 3 or 4 to be moderately infected, and ratings of 5 or 6 to be severely infected. Overall, mortality rates for uninfected and lightly infected trees were not significantly different (at the 66-percent confidence level). For individual species, such as grand fir, noble fir, subalpine fir, and Engelmann spruce, that were seldom found to be

Fifteen percent of conifers in eastern Oregon had mistletoe infection. Only 4 percent of those in western Oregon were infected.

Table 34—Conifers ≥5 inches diameter at breast height and those infected with dwarf mistletoe, by mistletoe severity rating and tree species

Species	All conifers Total	Infected trees Total	Infected trees Propor-tion	Infected trees SE	1-2 (minor) Propor-tion	1-2 (minor) SE	3-4 (moderate) Propor-tion	3-4 (moderate) SE	5-6 (severe) Propor-tion	5-6 (severe) SE
					Mistletoe severity rating					
	Thousand trees		– – – – – – – – – – – – – – – – *Percent* – – – – – – – – – – – – – – –							
Measured 1984-1997:										
Douglas-fir	1,218,263	39,512	3.2	0.3	1.5	0.1	1.0	0.1	0.7	0.1
Engelmann spruce	26,697	104	0.4	0.3	0.3	0.2	0.1	0.1	<0.1	<0.1
Grand fir	173,130	2,149	1.2	0.5	0.8	0.4	0.2	0.1	0.2	0.1
Lodgepole pine	296,193	93,170	31.5	1.9	11.4	0.8	13.1	1.0	6.9	0.8
Mountain hemlock	133,029	21,996	16.5	2.8	3.7	0.9	6.9	1.3	6.0	1.4
Noble fir	21,726	565	2.6	1.1	1.4	0.5	1.1	0.5	0.2	0.2
Pacific silver fir	89,615	10,881	12.1	3.1	5.6	1.2	5.4	1.7	1.2	0.4
Ponderosa pine	454,747	50,817	11.2	0.8	5.2	0.4	4.0	0.4	1.9	0.2
Shasta red fir	23,439	1,945	8.3	6.7	5.9	5.4	1.9	1.3	0.4	0.2
Sitka spruce	20,727	0	<0.1	<0.1	<0.1	<0.1	<0.1	<0.1	<0.1	<0.1
Subalpine fir	55,181	1,874	3.4	1.6	1.0	0.4	1.9	1.0	0.6	0.3
Sugar pine	11,084	94	0.8	0.5	0.7	0.5	0.1	0.1	<0.1	<0.1
Western hemlock	286,270	22,734	7.9	1.0	2.8	0.5	2.6	0.3	2.5	0.5
Western larch	34,485	5,191	15.1	2.1	7.4	1.0	3.9	0.6	3.8	1.2
White fir	174,756	13,697	7.8	1.4	3.6	0.6	2.9	0.6	1.3	0.4
Other pines	29,705	1,918	6.5	1.8	2.9	1.1	2.8	0.8	0.8	0.3
Other conifers	144,257	2,079	1.4	0.3	0.7	0.2	0.7	0.2	0.1	<0.1
All conifers	3,193,304	268,724	8.4	0.3	3.4	0.2	3.2	0.2	1.8	0.1
Measured 1995-2003:										
Douglas-fir	1,292,955	39,248	3.0	0.2	1.5	0.1	1.0	0.1	0.6	0.1
Engelmann spruce	27,221	357	1.3	1.0	1.0	1.0	0.1	<0.1	0.2	0.2
Grand fir	169,121	1,334	0.8	0.3	0.6	0.2	0.2	0.1	<0.1	<0.1
Lodgepole pine	289,787	97,111	33.5	2.0	13.7	1.0	14.8	1.1	5.0	0.6
Mountain hemlock	127,062	21,910	17.2	2.7	3.6	0.6	7.0	1.4	6.7	1.3
Noble fir	23,187	539	2.3	1.0	1.3	0.6	0.8	0.4	0.2	0.1
Pacific silver fir	90,334	12,787	14.2	3.4	5.6	1.2	7.1	2.1	1.5	0.5
Ponderosa pine	456,385	55,701	12.2	0.8	5.8	0.4	4.3	0.4	2.2	0.3
Shasta red fir	24,043	1,867	7.8	6.4	5.8	5.3	1.6	1.1	0.3	0.2
Sitka spruce	21,336	349	1.6	1.4	0.2	0.3	1.4	1.3	<0.1	<0.1
Subalpine fir	46,384	1,622	3.5	1.7	1.4	0.7	1.4	0.7	0.7	0.4
Sugar pine	9,082	5	0.1	<0.1	<0.1	<0.1	<0.1	<0.1	<0.1	<0.1
Western hemlock	275,408	29,763	10.8	1.3	3.8	0.6	4.0	0.7	3.0	0.5
Western larch	31,752	10,068	31.7	3.1	12.6	1.4	10.2	1.2	8.9	1.7
White fir	158,830	12,880	8.1	1.3	3.9	0.7	2.9	0.5	1.3	0.4
Other pines	25,119	1,129	4.5	1.5	1.8	0.7	1.7	0.7	1.0	0.5
Other conifers	159,944	1,812	1.1	0.2	0.5	0.1	0.3	0.1	0.1	<0.1
All conifers	3,227,948	288,482	8.9	0.4	3.7	0.2	3.5	0.2	1.7	0.1

SE = standard error.

Table 35—Conifers ≥5 inches diameter at breast height, and those infected with dwarf mistletoe, by mistletoe severity rating and tree species, eastern Oregon, 1995–2003

Tree species	All conifers Total	Infected trees Total	Proportion Percent	SE	Mistletoe severity rating 1-2 (minor) Total	Proportion Percent	SE	3-4 (moderate) Total	Proportion Percent	SE	5-6 (severe) Total	Proportion Percent	SE
	Thousand trees	*Thousand trees*	*Percent*		*Thousand trees*	*Percent*		*Thousand trees*	*Percent*		*Thousand trees*	*Percent*	
Douglas-fir	169,837	30,752	18.1	1.1	14,519	8.5	0.6	9,659	5.7	0.5	6,574	3.9	0.5
Engelmann spruce	25,694	357	1.4	1.0	277	1.1	1.0	26	0.1	0.1	54	0.2	0.2
Grand fir	128,742	765	0.6	0.2	598	0.5	0.2	153	0.1	0.1	14	<0.1	<0.1
Lodgepole pine	260,890	92,337	35.4	2.2	37,980	14.6	1.1	41,058	15.7	1.2	13,299	5.1	0.6
Mountain hemlock	57,195	8,542	14.9	3.4	2,502	4.4	1.1	3,200	5.6	1.5	2,840	5.0	1.6
Noble fir	3,961	0	0	0									
Pacific silver fir	10,362	0	0	0									
Ponderosa pine	438,186	55,580	12.7	0.9	26,272	6.0	0.4	19,455	4.4	0.4	9,853	2.2	0.3
Shasta red fir	14,277	33	0.2	0.1	14	0.1	0.1	10	0.1	0	9	0.1	0.1
Subalpine fir	39,392	674	1.7	1.4	206	0.5	0.4	320	0.8	0.7	148	0.4	0.4
Sugar pine	3,837	2	<0.1	<0.1	2	<0.1	<0.1						
Western hemlock	3,731	0	0	0									
Western larch	31,513	10,050	31.9	3.1	4,002	12.7	1.4	3,221	10.2	1.2	2,827	9.0	1.7
White fir	111,116	9,753	8.8	1.8	4,349	3.9	0.9	3,488	3.1	0.7	1,916	1.7	0.5
Other pines	10,924	274	2.5	1.4	64	0.6	0.4	73	0.7	0.4	137	1.3	0.8
Other conifers	48,587	927	2.5	0.7	530	1.1	0.3	300	0.6	0.2	97	0.2	0.1
All conifers	1,358,243	210,048	15.5	0.6	91,315	6.7	0.3	80,964	6.0	0.3	37,769	2.8	0.2

SE = standard error.

Table 36—Conifers ≥5 inches diameter at breast height, and those infected with dwarf mistletoe, by mistletoe severity rating and tree species, western Oregon, 1995–2003

Tree species	All conifers	Infected trees			Mistletoe severity rating								
					1-2 (minor)			3-4 (moderate)			5-6 (severe)		
	Total	Total	Proportion	SE	Total	Proportion	SE	Total	Proportion	SE	Total	Proportion	SE
	Thousand trees	Thousand trees	Percent		Thousand trees	Percent		Thousand trees	Percent		Thousand trees	Percent	
Douglas-fir	1,123,072	8,496	0.8	0.1	4,391	0.4	0.1	3,022	0.3	0.1	1,083	0.1	0
Engelmann spruce	1,527	0	0	0									
Grand fir	40,379	569	1.4	0.9	377	0.9	0.8	192	0.5	0.4			
Lodgepole pine	28,897	4,773	16.5	5.7	1,630	5.6	2.2	1,898	6.6	2.8	1,245	4.3	1.8
Mountain hemlock	69,867	13,367	19.1	4.0	2,011	2.9	0.6	5,712	8.2	2.2	5,644	8.1	1.9
Noble fir	19,226	538	2.8	1.2	304	1.6	0.7	195	1.0	0.4	39	0.2	0.2
Pacific silver fir	79,972	12,787	16.0	3.7	5,086	6.4	1.4	6,379	8.0	2.3	1,322	1.7	0.5
Ponderosa pine	18,199	121	0.7	0.3	91	0.5	0.3	12	0.1	0	18	0.1	0.1
Shasta red fir	9,766	1,834	18.8	14.1	1,376	14.1	11.8	384	3.9	2.4	74	0.8	0.4
Sitka spruce	21,336	349	1.6	1.4	52	0.2	0.3	297	1.4	1.3			
Subalpine fir	6,992	947	13.6	7.5	429	6.1	3.7	340	4.9	2.6	178	2.6	1.2
Sugar pine	5,244	4	0.1	0.1				4	0.1	0.1			
Western hemlock	271,677	29,763	11.0	1.3	10,568	3.9	0.6	11,052	4.1	0.7	8,143	3.0	0.5
Western larch	239	18	7.6	5.1	4	1.7	1.7	14	5.9	3.6			
White fir	47,714	3,118	6.6	1.2	1,868	3.9	0.8	1,079	2.3	0.6	171	0.4	0.1
Other pines	14,195	855	6.0	2.4	389	2.7	1.1	345	2.4	1.2	121	0.8	0.6
Other conifers	111,356	467	0.5	0.2	291	0.3	0.1	146	0.1	0	30	<0.1	<0.1
All conifers	1,869,659	78,006	4.2	0.4	28,869	1.5	0.2	31,068	1.7	0.2	18,069	1.0	0.1

SE = standard error.

Table 37—Average annual mortality of conifers ≥5 inches diameter at breast height and those infected with mistletoe, by species and region, 1984–2003

Tree species	All mortality		Mortality with mistletoe			
	Total	SE	Total	SE	Proportion	SE
	------ Thousand trees ------				Percent	
Eastern Oregon:						
Douglas-fir	1,947	205	553	98	28.4	3.8
Engelmann spruce	504	115	2	2	0.5	0.3
Grand fir	2,096	238	9	8	0.4	0.4
Lodgepole pine	4,125	350	1,354	186	32.8	3.5
Mountain hemlock	593	173	227	155	38.2	16.2
Noble fir	102	68	5	5	4.7	2.1
Pacific silver fir	219	75	30	29	13.7	10.3
Ponderosa pine	3,184	293	345	49	10.8	1.7
Shasta red fir	148	48				
Sitka spruce						
Subalpine fir	1,463	204	64	42	4.4	2.8
Sugar pine	12	7				
Western hemlock	5	2				
Western larch	332	55	97	25	29.2	6.3
White fir	1,593	228	150	49	9.4	3.0
Other pines	227	41	28	11	12.2	4.8
Other conifers	138	35	1	1	0.6	0.5
All conifers	16,688	741	2,864	288	17.2	1.5
Western Oregon:						
Douglas-fir	5,911	481	51	26	0.9	0.4
Engelmann spruce	34	12				
Grand fir	433	112	1	1	0.2	0.2
Lodgepole pine	372	81	36	15	9.6	4.1
Mountain hemlock	840	249	140	44	16.7	6.6
Noble fir	182	64	6	3	3.5	2.1
Pacific silver fir	1,155	158	153	48	13.3	3.5
Ponderosa pine	71	24				
Shasta red fir	46	22	27	20	60.0	21.2
Sitka spruce	104	40				
Subalpine fir	585	193	6	5	1.0	0.9
Sugar pine	171	55				
Western hemlock	1,898	285	282	62	14.8	3.5
Western larch	1	0				
White fir	234	43	25	21	10.7	8.0
Other pines	180	37	18	13	10.1	6.6
Other conifers	522	145			0	0
All conifers	12,740	720	747	105	5.9	0.8

Table 37—Average annual mortality of conifers ≥5 inches diameter at breast height and those infected with mistletoe, by species and region, 1984–2003 (continued)

Tree species	All mortality		Mortality with mistletoe			
	Total	SE	Total	SE	Proportion	SE
	– – – – – – Thousand trees – – – – – –				*– – – Percent – – –*	
All Oregon:						
Douglas-fir	7,858	522	604	101	7.7	1.3
Engelmann spruce	538	115	2	2	0.5	0.3
Grand fir	2,529	263	10	8	0.4	0.3
Lodgepole pine	4,497	359	1,390	187	30.9	3.2
Mountain hemlock	1,433	303	367	161	25.6	9.4
Noble fir	284	93	11	6	4.0	1.6
Pacific silver fir	1,375	175	184	56	13.4	3.4
Ponderosa pine	3,255	294	345	49	10.6	1.6
Shasta red fir	194	53	27	20	14.1	9.5
Sitka spruce	104	40				
Subalpine fir	2,048	281	70	42	3.4	2.0
Sugar pine	183	55				
Western hemlock	1,903	285	282	62	14.8	3.5
Western larch	333	55	97	25	29.1	6.3
White fir	1,828	232	175	53	9.6	2.8
Other pines	407	55	46	17	11.2	4.0
Other conifers	661	149	1	1	0.1	0.1
All conifers	29,428	1,030	3,611	306	12.3	1.0

SE = standard error.

Table 38—Average annual mortality volume of conifers ≥9 inches diameter at breast height and those infected with mistletoe, by species and region, 1984–2003

Tree species	All mortality		Mortality with mistletoe			
	Total	SE	Total	SE	Proportion	SE
	– – – – Million board feet – – – –				– – – Percent – – –	
Eastern Oregon:						
Douglas-fir	154	18	59	11	38.4	4.5
Engelmann spruce	75	20	1	0	0.7	0.6
Grand fir	209	22	4	3	1.8	1.3
Lodgepole pine	88	8	23	3	26.2	2.9
Mountain hemlock	81	33	39	30	48.3	18.5
Noble fir	29	27	1	1	2.1	0.1
Pacific silver fir	19	8	4	4	22.0	17.8
Ponderosa pine	196	20	15	3	7.6	1.5
Shasta red fir	18	6				
Sitka spruce						
Subalpine fir	58	9	2	1	2.6	2.2
Sugar pine	0	0				
Western hemlock	2	1				
Western larch	40	8	10	2	25.8	6.5
White fir	157	23	21	6	13.4	3.8
Other pines	25	6	3	1	10.7	5.6
Other conifers	3	1	0	0	8.8	8.7
All eastern Oregon	1,154	73	182	37	15.7	2.8
Western Oregon:						
Douglas-fir	637	56	16	6	2.6	0.9
Engelmann spruce	6	3				
Grand fir	32	7	1	1	2.8	2.8
Lodgepole pine	10	2	1	0	7.6	3.8
Mountain hemlock	78	36	8	4	10.3	6.7
Noble fir	33	11	4	2	11.4	6.0
Pacific silver fir	59	9	10	3	16.8	4.8
Ponderosa pine	7	5				
Shasta red fir	12	7	5	6	45.8	29.3
Sitka spruce	10	5				
Subalpine fir	12	5	0	0	0.4	0.4
Sugar pine	31	10			0	0
Western hemlock	172	24	47	12	27.1	6.0
Western larch	1	1				
White fir	31	6	2	1	5.3	2.7
Other pines	25	9	1	1	3.6	3.4
Other conifers	23	4			0	0
All western Oregon	1,179	81	94	16	8.0	1.3

Table 38—Average annual mortality volume of conifers ≥9 inches diameter at breast height and those infected with mistletoe, by species and region, 1984–2003 (continued)

Tree species	All mortality		Mortality with mistletoe			
	Total	SE	Total	SE	Proportion	SE
	– – – – *Million board feet* – – – –				– – – *Percent* – – –	
All Oregon:						
Douglas-fir	791	59	75	13	9.5	1.6
Engelmann spruce	80	20	1	0	0.7	0.5
Grand fir	240	23	5	3	1.9	1.2
Lodgepole pine	99	9	24	3	24.2	2.7
Mountain hemlock	159	49	47	30	29.7	14.7
Noble fir	62	29	4	2	7.0	3.6
Pacific silver fir	78	12	14	5	18.1	5.8
Ponderosa pine	203	21	15	3	7.3	1.4
Shasta red fir	30	9	5	6	18.4	15.9
Sitka spruce	10	5				
Subalpine fir	70	10	2	1	2.2	1.8
Sugar pine	31	10				
Western hemlock	174	24	47	12	26.8	5.9
Western larch	42	8	10	2	25.1	6.3
White fir	188	24	23	7	12.0	3.2
Other pines	49	11	4	2	7.2	3.4
Other conifers	26	4	0	0	1.1	1.1
All conifers	2,333	109	276	40	11.8	1.6

SE = standard error.

infected, there was not enough mortality of infected trees to make a reliable estimate. For tree species that had a large sample of infected trees to use, estimated mortality rates tended to increase with increasing severity of mistletoe infection. Except for the true firs and spruces, all species groups had significantly higher mortality rates in severely infected trees (at the 66-percent confidence level) compared to uninfected trees (fig. 13). Douglas-fir and all conifers as a group had significantly higher mortality at the moderately infected level. Overall, conifers with no mistletoe infections had an annual rate of mortality of 0.9 percent, conifers with moderate mistletoe infections had a mortality rate of 1.2 percent, and those with severe mistletoe infections died at a rate of 2.1 percent per year (fig. 13).

Rates of mistletoe infection were found to differ by ownership across the state. About 4 percent of conifers on privately owned forest land were found to be infected with dwarf mistletoe. About 10 percent of conifers on public forest lands

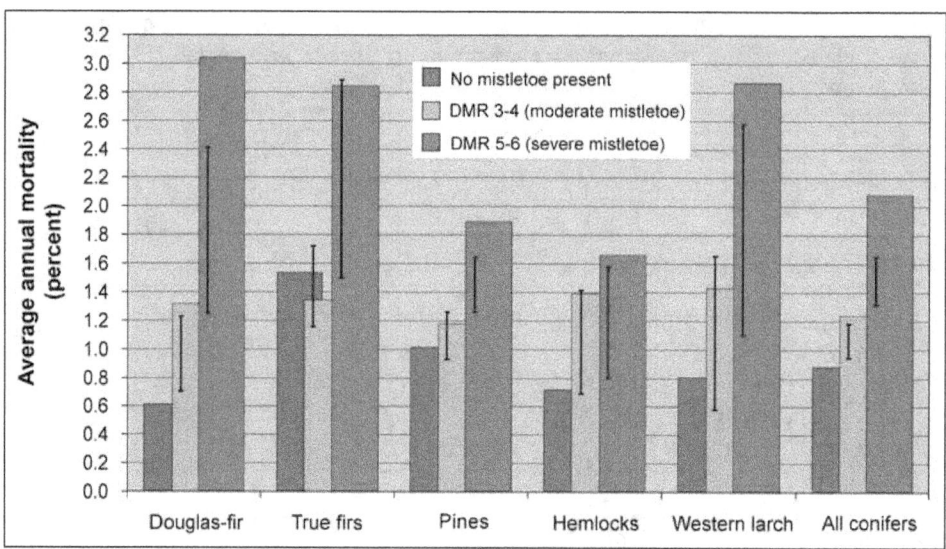

Figure 13—Average annual mortality rate of conifers ≥5 inches diameter at breast height without dwarf mistletoe infection compared to conifers with moderate to severe infection, 1984–2003. Error bars indicate the standard error of the difference between the mortality rate of infected trees and the mortality rate of uninfected trees. DMR = dwarf mistletoe severity rating.

were infected. National forest lands had the highest rate of infection with 12 percent (table 39). These differences are likely due to differences in species composition and management objectives. Private landowners have a strong economic motivation to harvest trees that are not rapidly growing or are at risk of dying. Also, national forests have a higher proportion of species that are commonly infected such as lodgepole pine, mountain hemlock, and western larch.

Animal Damage

Trees in Oregon forests are damaged by a variety of animals. Seedlings are sometimes eaten by livestock, deer, elk, or rodents. Black bears (*Ursus americanus* Linn.) and porcupines (*Erethizon dorsatum* Linn.) will strip bark from portions of trees to feed on the cambium. Seedlings and saplings may be trampled by livestock or elk.

Probably, most of the mortality caused by animals is done by herbivores browsing seedlings and small saplings. Unfortunately it was not possible to examine mortality of these small trees because the sampling protocols used to measure the plots either excluded seedlings that would not survive or merely counted their numbers without detailed information as to their condition.

Table 39—Conifers ≥5 inches diameter at breast height, and conifers infected with mistletoe, by ownership and mistletoe severity 1995–2003

Ownership	All conifers		Any infection				Mistletoe severity rating					
							1-2 (minor)		3-4 (moderate)		5-6 (severe)	
	Total	SE	Total	SE	Propor-tion	SE	Total	SE	Total	SE	Total	SE
	— — — — Thousand trees — — — —		— — — — Thousand trees — — — —		Percent		— — — — — — Thousand trees — — — — — —					
Bureau of Land Management	286,580	12,012	5,046	1,705	1.2	0.4	2,391	758	1,481	735	1,146	429
National forest	1,768,805	23,029	232,988	10,150	12.2	0.5	94,676	4,127	92,721	5,007	45,592	2,980
Other public	118,909	10,783	2,585	1,247	1.6	0.8	1,476	956	894	440	193	160
All public owners	2,174,295	28,123	240,619	10,367	9.7	0.4	98,543	4,304	95,096	5,080	46,932	3,015
Private, nonindustrial	344,921	16,847	14,744	2,369	3.4	0.5	6,111	1,056	5,520	1,262	2,857	853
Private, industrial	708,732	26,894	33,110	4,659	3.9	0.5	15,530	2,871	11,416	2,394	6,050	1,418
All private owners	1,053,653	31,554	47,854	5,195	3.8	0.4	21,641	3,051	16,936	2,703	8,906	1,646
All owners	3,227,948	41,975	288,473	11,593	7.6	0.3	120,184	5,275	112,032	5,755	55,838	3,433

SE = standard error.

77

About 0.7 percent of conifers were found to be damaged by animals, whereas just 0.1 percent of hardwoods were damaged. Two-thirds of the damage to conifers was attributed to unknown animals. Of individual species, only whitebark pine and ponderosa pine had damage on more than 1 percent of the trees. Porcupine damage was recorded on 2.5 percent of the ponderosa pine, or about 11 million trees state-wide. Porcupines accounted for 90 percent of the animal damage to ponderosa pine and 59 percent of the animal damage to all conifers (table 40).

It is likely than some animal damage goes undetected or is misidentified by forest inventory crews. Porcupine damage in ponderosa pine is relatively easy to identify because the animals strip the bark at a preferred stem diameter. The resulting death of the tree's leader and the upturning of nearby branches into new leaders makes a distinctive candelabra pattern that can be recognized for years. Damage by other animals is harder to recognize. In spring when bears are recently out of hibernation and much of their forage is not yet available, they are known to strip the bark from trees to eat the cambium underneath. Groups of trees killed by bears are commonly noticed by aerial survey crews in the Oregon Coast Range and Western Cascades, yet this damage is seldom recorded on inventory plots. It is possible that when a tree is damaged by bear more than a few years before a plot is measured that inventory crews cannot discern whether the bark was stripped off by an animal or if it fell off of wood that was already dead for some other reason.

The Oregon Department of Forestry conducts yearly aerial surveys to detect damage from black bears in western Oregon. From 1996 to 2006, the amount of area observed to have bear damage averaged 27,000 acres per year (fig. 14). The largest number of acres mapped in that time was 48,813 in 2006. These should be considered acres with bear damage and not acres of bear damage. Not every tree in a mapped area will have damage. Bear damage was most common in the Oregon Coast Range and Western Cascade ecosections (fig. 15).

Table 40—Trees ≥5 inches diameter at breast height damaged by animals and proportion damaged, by tree species and animal, 1995–2003

Tree species	All live trees Total	Any animal damage Total	Any animal damage Proportion	Any animal damage SE	Unknown animal Proportion	Unknown animal SE	Porcupines Proportion	Porcupines SE	Bear Proportion	Bear SE	All other animals Proportion	All other animals SE
	Thousand trees						-- *Percent* --					
Douglas-fir	1,292,955	4,944	0.4	0.1	0.1	<0.1	<0.1	<0.1	0.2	<0.1	<0.1	<0.1
Engelmann spruce	27,221	41	0.2	0.1	0.2	0.1						
Grand fir	169,121	471	0.3	0.2	0.2	0.1	<0.1	<0.1	<0.1	<0.1	0.1	0.1
Lodgepole pine	289,787	1,956	0.7	0.1	0.1	<0.1	0.4	0.1	0.1	<0.1	<0.1	<0.1
Mountain hemlock	127,062	110	0.1	0	0.1	<0.1			<0.1	<0.1		
Noble fir	23,187	71	0.3	0.2	0.2	0.1			0.1	0.2		
Pacific silver fir	90,334	191	0.2	0.1	<0.1	<0.1	<0.1	<0.1	0.2	0.1		
Ponderosa pine	456,385	12,672	2.8	0.3	0.3	0.1	2.5	0.3			<0.1	<0.1
Shasta red fir	24,043	60	0.3	0.2	0.3	0.2						
Sitka spruce	21,336	78	0.4	0.3	0.3	0.1			0.1	0.1	0.3	0.3
Subalpine fir	46,384	213	0.5	0.2	0.1	<0.1			<0.1	<0.1	0.2	0.1
Sugar pine	9,082	37	0.4	0.2	0.1	<0.1	0.3	0.2				
Western hemlock	275,408	683	0.2	0.1	0.1	<0.1			0.1	0.1	<0.1	<0.1
Western larch	31,752	10	0	0	0	<0.1						
Western white pine	10,722	87	0.8	0.5	0.6	0.4	0.2	0.2				
White fir	158,830	698	0.4	0.1	0.1	<0.1	0.3	0.1			<0.1	<0.1
Whitebark pine	7,839	92	1.2	0.6	0.7	0.5	0.5	0.3				
Other conifers	166,502	752	0.5	0.2	0.3	0.2	<0.1	<0.1	0.1	<0.1	<0.1	<0.1
All conifers	3,227,948	23,167	0.7	0.1	0.2	<0.1	0.4	<0.1	0.1	<0.1	<0.1	<0.1
All hardwoods	573,094	785	0.1	0.1	0.1	0.1	<0.1	<0.1	<0.1	<0.1	<0.1	<0.1

SE = standard error.

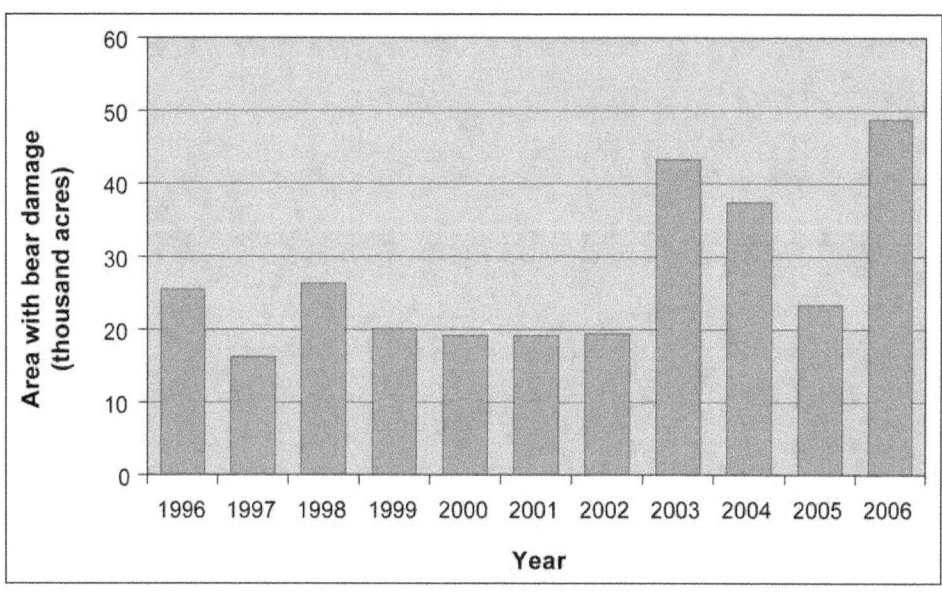

Figure 14—Area with bear damage detected by aerial survey 1996–2006. Source: USDA FS 2007.

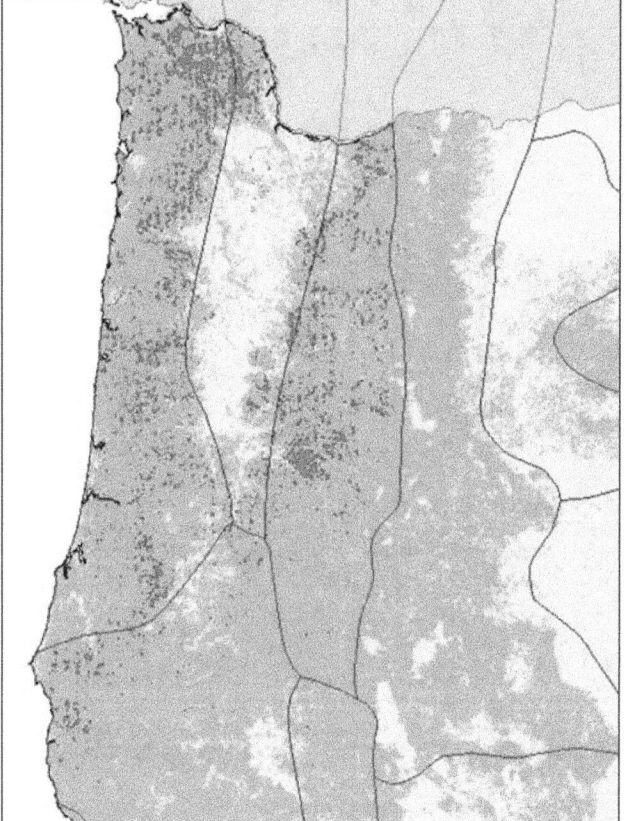

Figure 15—Distribution of bear damage detected by aerial survey 1998–2003. Mapped bear damage areas have been slightly enlarged on the map to make them visible at this scale. Source: USDA FS 2007.

Conclusion

In a general sense, the impacts of insects and diseases result from the reactions of these organisms to their environments. The characteristics of Oregon's forests have been changing for over a century. The current state of our forests has been shaped by changes in human activity and climate as well as insect and disease activity. The frequency and severity of insect and disease outbreaks has increased (Campbell and Liegel 1996). These outbreaks are a response of the insects and diseases to new opportunities. Harvesting in western Oregon has replaced many native stands with Douglas-fir plantations of less species and age diversity. In eastern Oregon, harvesting has reduced the number of large old pines. Aggressive fire suppression in the east has allowed the proportion and density of relatively shade-tolerant grand fir and Douglas-fir to increase in ponderosa pine stands (Hessburg et al. 1994). Fire exclusion, grazing, and climate are thought to be responsible for the acreage covered by western juniper forest increasing by over a million acres since the 1930s (Azuma et al. 2005). There are new insects and diseases in Oregon's forests that were not here a century ago, and there will likely be new ones introduced in the next century. White pine blister rust, Port-Orford-cedar root disease, and the balsam woolly adelgid have already altered the ecosystems into which they have spread. Sudden oak death has the potential to be a serious disease in southwestern Oregon.

The above factors illustrate that the overall characteristics of Oregon's forests today are unlike those that existed in the past. The Oregon forests of the future may be very different than what we have today. Forests with high levels of insect and disease activity may be forests transitioning to some new condition. The concepts of healthy and unhealthy are human-derived values. Whether the current conditions should be considered unhealthy or not depends on whether the forest will be able to continue providing the benefits that we value. The above factors also illustrate that humans can influence the state of forest conditions. Whether or not our forests continue to provide the wood fiber, recreation, scenery, biodiversity, and wildlife habitat that we value will depend in large part on how we decide to manage and protect our forests.

Names of Trees

Common name	Scientific name
Softwoods:	
Douglas-fir	*Pseudotsuga menziesii* (Mirb.) Franco
Engelmann spruce	*Picea engelmannii* Parry ex Engelm.
Grand fir	*Abies grandis* (Dougl. ex D. Don) Lindl.
Incense-cedar	*Calocedrus decurrens* (Torr.) Florin.
Jeffrey pine	*Pinus jeffreyi* Grev. & Balf.
Knobcone pine	*Pinus attenuata* Lemmon
Lodgepole pine	*Pinus contorta* Dougl. ex Loud.
Mountain hemlock	*Tsuga mertensiana* (Bong.) Carr.
Noble fir	*Abies procera* Rehd.
Pacific silver fir	*Abies amabilis* Dougl. ex Forbes.
Pacific yew	*Taxus brevifolia* Nutt.
Ponderosa pine	*Pinus ponderosa* Dougl. ex Laws.
Port-Orford-cedar	*Chamaecyparis lawsoniana* (A. Murr.) Parl.
Redwood	*Sequoia sempervirens* (D. Don) Endl.
Scotch pine	*Pinus sylvestris* L.
Shasta red fir	*Abies shastensis* (Lemmon)
Sitka spruce	*Picea sitchensis* (Bong.) Carr.
Subalpine fir	*Abies lasiocarpa* (Hook.) Nutt.
Sugar pine	*Pinus lambertiana* Dougl.
Western hemlock	*Tsuga heterophylla* (Raf.) Sarg.
Western juniper	*Juniperus occidentalis* Hook.
Western larch	*Larix occidentalis* Nutt.
Western redcedar	*Thuja plicata* Donn ex D. Don
Western white pine	*Pinus monticola* Dougl. ex D. Don
White fir	*Abies concolor* (Gord. & Glend.) Lindl. ex Hildebr.
Whitebark pine	*Pinus albicaulis* Engelm.
Hardwoods:	
Apple	*Malus spp.*
Black cottonwood	*Populus balsamifera* L. ssp. *trichocarpa* (Torr. & A. Gray ex Hook.) Brayshaw
Bigleaf maple	*Acer macrophyllum* Pursh.
California black oak	*Quercus kelloggii* Newb.
California-laurel	*Umbellularia californica* (Hook. & Arn.) Nutt.
Canyon live oak	*Quercus chrysolepis* Liebm.
Cherry	*Prunus* spp.
Golden chinkapin	*Chrysolepis chrysophylla* (Douglas ex Hook.) Hjelmqvist var. *chrysophylla*
Oregon ash	*Fraxinus latifolia* Benth.
Oregon white oak	*Quercus garryana* Dougl. ex Hook.
Pacific madrone	*Arbutus menziesii* Pursh.
Quaking aspen	*Populus tremuloides* Michx.
Red alder	*Alnus rubra* Bong.
Tanoak	*Lithocarpus densiflorus* (Hook. & Arn.) Rehd.
White alder	*Alnus rhombifolia* Nutt.
Willow	*Salix* spp.

Acknowledgments

Thanks to David Azuma, David Bridgewater, Sally Campbell, Glenn Christensen, Greg Filip, Olaf Kuegler, Alison Nelson, and Iral Ragenovich for their reviews and assistance with this report. My thanks are also extended to the aerial survey pilots and observers, and the forest inventory crewmembers and contractors who braved long days, weather, brush, and rough terrain to collect the information used in this report.

Metric Equivalents

1 acre = 0.405 hectare

1 acre = 4046.86 square meters

1,000 acres = 404.7 hectares

1,000 cubic feet = 28.3 cubic meters

1 cubic foot per acre = 0.07 cubic meter per hectare

1 foot = 0.3048 meters

1 inch = 2.54 centimeters

1 mile = 1.609 kilometers

Literature Cited

Aho, P.E. 1966. Defect estimation for grand fir, Engelmann spruce, Douglas-fir and western larch in the Blue Mountains of Oregon and Washington. Portland, OR: U.S. Department of Agriculture, Forest Service, Pacific Northwest Forest and Range Experiment Station. 26 p.

Aho, P.E.; Simonski, P. 1975. Defect estimation for white fir in the Fremont National Forest. Res Pap. PNW-196. Portland, OR: U.S. Department of Agriculture, Forest Service, Pacific Northwest Forest and Range Experiment Station. 9 p.

Amman, G.D.; McGregor, M.D.; Dolph, R.E., Jr. 1989. Mountain pine beetle. Forest Insect and Disease Leaflet 2. Portland, OR: U.S. Department of Agriculture, Forest Service, Pacific Northwest Region State and Private Forestry. 11 p.

Azuma, D.L.; Hiserote, B.A.; Dunham, P.A. 2005. The western juniper resource of eastern Oregon, in 1999. Resour. Bull. PNW-RB-249. Portland, OR: U.S. Department of Agriculture, Forest Service, Pacific Northwest Research Station. 18 p.

Bailey, R.G. 2004. Bailey's ecoregions and subregions of the United States, Puerto Rico, and the U.S. Virgin Islands [Digital Map]. Reston, VA: U.S. Department of Agriculture, Forest Service.

Bechtold, W.A.; Patterson, P.L. 2005. The enhanced Forest Inventory and Analysis Program–national sampling design and estimation procedures. Gen. Tech. Rep. SRS-GTR-80. Asheville, NC: U.S. Department of Agriculture, Forest Service, Southern Research Station. 85 p.

Bergoffen, W.W. 1976. 100 years of federal forestry. Agric. Info. Bull. 402 Washington, DC: U.S. Department of Agriculture, Forest Service. 200 p.

Bull, E.L.; Parks, C.G.; Torgersen, T.R. 1997. Trees and logs important to wildlife in the interior Columbia River basin. Gen. Tech. Rep. PNW-GTR-391. Portland, OR: U.S. Department of Agriculture, Forest Service, Pacific Northwest Research Station. 55 p.

Burns, R.M.; Honkala, B.H. 1990. Silvics of North America. Agric. Handb. 654. Washington, DC: U.S. Department of Agriculture, Forest Service. 675 p.

Campbell, S.; Azuma, D.; Weyermann, D. 2002. Forests of western Oregon: an overview. Gen.Tech. Rep. PNW-GTR-525. Portland, OR: U.S. Department of Agriculture, Forest Service, Pacific Northwest Research Station. 27 p.

Campbell, S.; Azuma, D.; Weyermann, D. 2003. Forests of eastern Oregon: an overview. Gen.Tech. Rep. PNW-GTR-578. Portland, OR: U.S. Department of Agriculture, Forest Service, Pacific Northwest Research Station. 31 p.

Campbell, S.; Dunham, P.; Azuma, D. 2004. Timber resource statistics for Oregon. Resour. Bull. PNW-RB-242. Portland, OR: U.S. Department of Agriculture, Forest Service, Pacific Northwest Research Station. 67 p.

Campbell, S.; Liegel, L., tech. cords. 1996. Disturbance and forest health in Oregon and Washington. Gen. Tech. Rep. PNW-GTR-381. Portland, OR: U.S. Department of Agriculture, Forest Service, Pacific Northwest Research Station, Pacific Northwest Region; Oregon Department of Forestry; Washington Department of Natural Resources. 105 p.

Cochran, W.G. 1977. Sampling techniques. 3rd ed. New York: John Wiley and Sons. 413 p.

DeMars, C.J., Jr.; Roettgering, B.H. 1982. Western pine beetle. Forest Insect & Disease Leaflet 1. Berkley, CA: US. Department of Agriculture, Forest Service, Pacific Southwest Forest and Range Experiment Station. 9 p.

Donnegan, J.A.; Campbell, S.; Azuma, D.; tech. coords. [In press]. Oregon's Forest Resources: Forest Inventory and Analysis, 2001-2005. Resour. Bull. Portland, OR: U.S. Department of Agriculture, Forest Service, Pacific Northwest Research Station.

Filip, G.M.; Schmitt, C.L. 1990. Rx for *Abies*: silvicultural options for diseased firs in Oregon and Washington. Gen. Tech. Rep. PNW-252. Portland, OR: U.S. Department of Agriculture, Forest Service, Pacific Northwest Research Station. 34 p.

Geils, B.W.; Cibrián Tovar, J.; Moody, B., tech. cords. 2002. Mistletoes of North American conifers. Gen. Tech. Rep. RMRS-GTR-98. Ogden UT: U.S. Department of Agriculture, Forest Service, Rocky Mountain Research Station. 123 p.

Goheen, E.M.; Willhite, E.A. 2006. Field guide to common diseases and insect pests of Oregon and Washington conifers. R6-NR-FID-PR-01-06. Portland, OR: U.S. Department of Agriculture, Forest Service, Pacific Northwest Region. 327 p.

Hawksworth, F.G. 1977. The six class dwarf mistletoe rating system. Gen. Tech. Rep. RM-48. Fort Collins, CO: U.S. Department of Agriculture, Forest Service, Rocky Mountain Forest and Range Experiment Station. 7 p.

Hessburg, P.F.; Mitchell, R.G.; Filip, G.M. 1994. Historical and current roles of insects and pathogens in eastern Oregon and Washington forested landscapes. Gen. Tech. Rep. PNW-GTR-327. Portland, OR: U.S. Department of Agriculture, Forest Service, Pacific Northwest Research Station. 72 p.

Johnson, M.D. 1998. Region 6 inventory and monitoring system: field procedures for the current vegetation survey. Version 2.03. Portland, OR: U.S. Department of Agriculture, Forest Service. 143 p.

Johnson, M.D. 2001. Region 6 inventory and monitoring system: field procedures for the current vegetation survey. Version 2.04. Portland, OR: U.S. Department of Agriculture, Forest Service. 151 p.

Kanaskie, A.; Baer D. 1994. Occurrence and impact of laminated root rot on nonfederal conifer timberlands in western Oregon. Oregon Department of Forestry Forest Health Report. On file with: U.S. Department of Agriculture, Forest Service, Pacific Northwest Forest Inventory and Analysis, 620 SW Main, Suite 400, Portland, OR 97205.

Kanaskie, A.; Osterbauer, N.; McWilliams, M.; Goheen, E.; Hansen, E.; Sutton, W. 2006. Eradication of *Phytophthora ramorum* in Oregon forests—status after 3 years. In: Frankel, S.J.; Shea, P.J.; Haverty, M.I., tech. coords. Proceedings of the sudden oak death second science symposium: the state of our knowledge. Gen. Tech. Rep. PSW-GTR-196. Albany, CA: U.S. Department of Agriculture, Forest Service, Pacific Southwest Research Station: 489–490.

Keen, F.P. 1952. Insect enemies of western forests. Misc. Publ. 273 (revised). Washington, DC: U.S. Department of Agriculture. 280 p.

Kegley, S.J.; Livingston, R.L.; Gibson, K.E. 1997. Pine engraver, *Ips pini* (Say), in the Western United States. Forest Insect & Disease Leaflet 122. Missoula, MT: U.S. Department of Agriculture, Forest Service, Cooperative Forestry and Forest Health Protection, Northern Region. 5 p.

Kuegler, O. 2005. User guide to the OK Tabling Program version 0.9d. On file with: U.S. Department of Agriculture, Forest Service, Pacific Northwest Forest Inventory and Analysis, 620 SW Main, Suite 400, Portland, OR 97205.

Maguire, D.A.; Kanaskie, A.; Voelker, W.; Johnson, R.; Johnson, G. 2002. Growth of young Douglas-fir plantations across a gradient in Swiss needle cast severity. Western Journal of Applied Forestry. 17(2): 86–95.

Mai, J.A.; Mark, W.; Fischer, L.; Jirka, A. 2006. Aerial and ground surveys for mapping the distribution of *Phytophthora ramorum* in California. In: Frankel, S.J.; Shea, P.J.; Haverty, M.I., tech. coords. Proceedings of the sudden oak death second science symposium: the state of our knowledge. Gen. Tech. Rep. PSW-GTR-196. Albany, CA: U.S. Department of Agriculture, Forest Service, Pacific Southwest Research Station: 345–360.

McDonald G.I.; Zambino P.; Sniezko, R.A. 2004. Breeding rust-resistant five-needle pines in the Western United States: lessons from the past and a look to the future. In: Breeding and genetic resources of five-needle pines: growth, adaptability, and pest resistance. Fort Collins, CO: U.S. Department of Agriculture, Forest Service, Rocky Mountain Research Station: 28–50.

Nelson, A.S. 2005. Forest health highlights in Oregon, 2003. R6-NR-FID-TP-05-04. Portland, OR: U.S. Department of Agriculture, Forest Service. 16 p.

Overhulser, D.L.; Ragenovich, I. R.; McWilliams, M; Willhite, E.A. 2004. Balsam woolly adelgid occurrence on true fir in Oregon. Pest Management Report. Salem, OR: Oregon Department of Forestry. 7 p.

U.S. Department of Agriculture, Forest Service [USDA FS]. 1995. Field instructions for the inventory of western Oregon, Pacific Resources Inventory, Monitoring, and Evaluation Program, Pacific Northwest Research Station, U.S. Department of Agriculture, Forest Service. http://www.fs.fed.us/pnw/fia/local-resources/pdf/field_manuals/or/1995-97_field_manual_oregon.pdf. (August 2007).

U.S. Department of Agriculture, Forest Service [USDA FS]. 1998. Field instructions for the inventory of eastern Oregon. Pacific Resources Inventory, Monitoring, and Evaluation Program, Pacific Northwest Research Station, U.S. Department of Agriculture, Forest Service. http://www.fs.fed.us/pnw/fia/local-resources/pdf/field_manuals/or/1998_eor_timberland_pdf_versiontry6.pdf. (August 2007).

U.S. Department of Agriculture, Forest Servicce [USDA FS]. 2007. Forest insect and disease aerial detection survey, 1980–2006. Forest Health Protection, State and Private Forestry, Pacific Northwest Region, Forest Service, U.S. Department of Agriculture; Washington Department of Natural Resources; Oregon Department of Forestry. [Vector digital data]. http://www.fs.fed.us/r6/nr/fid/as/index.shtml. (August 2007).

Waddell K.L; Hiserote, B. 2005. The PNW-FIA integrated database [database on CD]. Version 2.0. Portland, OR: Forest Inventory and Analysis Program, Pacific Northwest Research Station. http://www.fs.fed.us/pnw/fia/publications/data/data.shtml. (accessed August 2006).

Glossary

Bureau of Land Management land—Land administered by the U.S. Department of the Interior, Bureau of Land Management.

county and municipal lands—Lands owned by county and other municipalities.

forest industry lands—Lands owned by companies that grow timber for industrial use. Includes companies both with and without wood processing plants.

forest land—Land at least 10-percent stocked with live trees, or land that had this minimum tree stocking in the past and is not currently developed for nonforest use. The minimum area recognized is 1 acre.

forest types—Stands are assigned a pure softwood, pure hardwood, softwood-hardwood mix, or hardwood-softwood mix. Stands with 70 percent or more of the stocking in live softwood trees are classified as pure softwood types and are assigned the type name of the softwood species with the greatest stocking among all softwoods on the condition class plot. Stands with 70 percent or more of the stocking in live hardwood trees are classified as pure hardwood types and are assigned the type name of the hardwood species with the greatest stocking among all hardwoods on the condition class plot. Mixed species types are assigned if softwood stocking is between 31 and 69 percent total stocking on the plot: stands with 50 to 69 percent of the stocking in live softwood trees are classed as softwood-hardwood types, and receive a type name that includes the softwood species with the greatest softwood stocking, followed by the hardwood species with the greatest hardwood stocking; stands with 51 to 69 percent of the stocking in live hardwood trees are classed as hardwood-softwood types, and receive a type name that includes the hardwood species with the greatest hardwood stocking, followed by the softwood species with the greatest softwood stocking. For ease in reporting, the secondary forest type will be identified after a slash as "softwood" or "hardwood" in the summary tables.

hardwoods—Nonconiferous trees, usually broadleaved. See "Names of Trees" for a list of hardwood species in this report.

national forest lands—Federal lands that have been designated by Executive order or statute as national forest or purchase units and other lands under the administration of the Forest Service, U.S. Department of Agriculture, including experimental areas and Bankhead-Jones Title III lands.

Native American lands—Tribal lands, and allotted lands held in trust by the federal government. Native American lands are grouped with farmer and miscellaneous private lands as other private lands.

nonforest land—Land that has never supported forests or formerly was forested and currently is developed for nonforest uses. Included are lands used for agricultural crops, Christmas tree farms, cottonwood plantations, improved pasture, residential areas, city parks, constructed roads, operating railroads and their right-of-way clearings, powerline and pipeline clearings, streams more than 30 feet wide, and 1- to 40-acre areas of water classified by the Bureau of the Census, U.S. Department of Commerce, as land. If intermingled in forest areas, unimproved roads and other nonforest strips must be more than 120 feet wide, and clearings or other areas must be 1 acre or larger to qualify as nonforest land.

nonstocked areas—Timberland less than 10-percent stocked with live trees. Recent clearcuts scheduled for planting are classified as nonstocked area.

other private lands—Private lands not owned by forest industry. Native American lands, farmer-owned lands, and miscellaneous private lands are included.

other public lands—Lands administered by public agencies other than the U.S. Department of Agriculture, Forest Service and U.S. Department of the Interior, Bureau of Land Management. Other public lands do not include Native American lands, which are included with other private lands.

poletimber trees—Live growing-stock trees of commercial species that are 5.0 inches in diameter at breast height (d.b.h.) or larger but smaller than sawtimber trees.

sapling and seedling trees—Live trees of commercial species that are less than 5.0 inches in d.b.h. with a minimum height of 6.0 inches and have no diseases, defects, or deformities likely to prevent their becoming poletimber trees. Saplings have a minimum diameter of 1.0 inch.

sawtimber trees—Live softwood trees of commercial species at least 9.0 inches in d.b.h. and live hardwood trees of commercial species at least 11.0 inches in d.b.h. At least 25 percent of the board-foot volume in a sawtimber tree must be free from defect. Softwood trees must contain at least one 12-foot saw log with a top diameter of not less than 7 inches outside bark; hardwood trees must contain at least one 8-foot saw log with a top diameter of not less than 9 inches outside bark.

Scribner rule—The common board-foot log rule used locally in eastern Oregon to determine sawtimber volume. Scribner volume is estimated in terms of 16-foot logs for softwoods and hardwoods. See "Sawtimber trees" for utilization limits.

site index—A measure of the productivity of forest land expressed as the average height of dominant and codominant trees at a specified age.

softwoods—Coniferous trees, usually evergreen, with needles or scalelike leaves. See "Names of Trees" for a list of softwood species in this report.

state lands—Lands owned by states or administered by state agencies.

www.ingramcontent.com/pod-product-compliance
Lightning Source LLC
Chambersburg PA
CBHW080316290526
45790CB00005B/2066